Soulpreneurs

Soulpreneurs

Live Your Purpose
Lift Your Platform
and
Leap into Prosperity

Yvette Luciano

HAY HOUSE, INC.
Carlsbad, California • New York City
London • Sydney • Johannesburg
Vancouver • New Delhi

Published and distributed in Australia by: Hay House Australia Pty. Ltd.: www.hayhouse.com.au
Published and distributed in the United States by: Hay House, Inc.: www.hayhouse.com
Published and distributed in the United Kingdom by: Hay House UK, Ltd.: www.hayhouse.co.uk
Distributed in Canada by: Raincoast Books: www.raincoast.com
Published in India by: Hay House Publishers India: www.hayhouse.co.in

Internal Design by Rhett Nacson
Typeset by Bookhouse
Illustrations by Sarah Wilder
Author photo by Michelle Swan
Edited by Margie Tubbs

ISBN: 978-1-4019-5085-9
Digital ISBN: 978-1-4019-5086-6

10 9 8 7 6 5 4 3 2 1
1st edition, February 2018

Printed in the United States of America

In loving honour of Louise Hay,
the original Soulpreneur

Walk with the dreamers, the believers,
the courageous, the cheerful, the planners, the
doers, the successful people with their heads
in the clouds and their feet on the ground.
Let their spirit ignite a fire within you to leave
this world better than when you found it.

– **Wilferd A. Peterson**

Contents

Foreword ix
A Message from Yvette xi
Preface xv
Introduction 1

part ONE
CLARITY

1 The Real Reason You Are Here 11
2 Clarity, Focus, Goals 23
3 From Day Job to Dream Life 37
4 Going Back to the Future 51
5 Be Your Own Business Guru 56
6 The Greatest Career Investment 78
7 Your Audience Awaits 105

part TWO
COURAGE

8 Step into Your True Power and Potential 127
9 The Path to Abundance and Prosperity 147
10 Shining in Your Sensitivity 172
11 Expressing Your Creativity 189

part THREE
PLATFORM

12 Leading with Love and Light 199
13 Income, Offerings and Operations 204
14 Your Beautiful Brand 220
15 Embracing the Digital World 235
16 PR, Media and Positive Influencers 254
17 Writing and Speaking with the World 264

Closing Notes 291
Acknowledgements 294

Foreword

I travelled to Australia in 2015 for a three-city speaking tour hosted by Yvette Luciano. I'd never met Yvette and I barely knew anything about her work, but for some reason I felt compelled to travel across the world to collaborate with her.

Yvette's enthusiasm, passion and commitment gave me the confidence to embark on a new adventure. From the moment I landed in Australia, I felt deeply cared for and celebrated by Yvette and her team. Over the course of those two weeks we spent a lot of time together on aeroplanes, backstage in green rooms and in auditoriums with hundreds of people. By the end of the tour I said to my husband, "I love Yvette. We **must** do this again." This began a collaboration that will last a lifetime.

Not only do I consider Yvette my business partner, but I also consider her a dear friend. Over the years we've become close as we grow personally, professionally and spiritually. I'm deeply proud of Yvette and her divine contribution to the world.

Yvette is the perfect guide for spiritual entrepreneurs who want to live and lead from a place of purpose. In her new book,

Soulpreneurs, she offers the pathway to success: practical expertise merged with spiritual faith.

Soulpreneurs reconnects you to why you are here, who you are here to serve and gives you the map to make it happen.

Let Yvette's passion, professional experiences and personal transformations ignite the Soulpreneur within you.

It's time to step into your true power and purpose.

Gabrielle Bernstein

#1 *New York Times* bestselling author of
The Universe Has Your Back

A Message from Yvette

So, you want to be a Soulpreneur? Come a little closer and I'll share a secret that your soul has been waiting to hear. C'mon in. Closer.

Here it is ... **Soulpreneur magic has been within you all along!**

It's been there, waiting for this moment, waiting for this book to land in your miracle-working hands. This book, this page, is the beginning of one of the most intimate and significant relationships you will ever have: the relationship between you and the soul of your business, your mission, your art, your music and your purpose.

You **do** know that she has been there all along, right? You **have** felt something deep inside, haven't you? Something yearning to be unleashed. Something urging you to become who you were born to be. To be seen, heard, set free.

And so here it is ...

Congratulations on saying '**yes**' to your soul's calling, for saying '**yes**' to the people in the world who need you to rise up.

Whether teaching yoga, playing music, writing books or hosting healing sessions, let's unleash that **something** within you.

Your angels are jumping with joy that this book is in your hands, because it means you've truly decided to live your purpose, lift your platform and leap into prosperity. And I'm jumping with joy alongside them, because I know exactly how it feels to make that decision.

Even though this is your first **official** step as a Soulpreneur, you'll soon discover you have been taking steps all along. Even if they felt like sideways or backward steps, every moment in your career and life has been part of your Soulpreneur journey:

- *Every life experience*
- *Every dreary day job*
- *Every exciting promotion at work*
- *Every heartbreak*
- *Every success celebration*
- *Every failed exam*
- *Every time you laughed so hard you held your belly*
- *Every night you cried on the cold hard floor*
- *Every time you fell in love*
- *Every time you were told to stop being so sensitive*
- *Every scary doctor's appointment*
- *Every time you felt good about helping a friend*
- *Every crazy music concert*
- *Every favourite book or film*

All these moments were stepping stones on the way to becoming the Soulpreneur you were born to be. The laughs, the tears, the highs, the lows and the lessons along the way all have meaning. All are part of this learning curve and path to who you are, who you most definitely are not, and why your soul chose this body, these circumstances and this lifetime to do the work you are here to do.

And so it begins. Let's light up your career and life, so that you can illuminate the way for others in this world.

It's time to make an abundant living by doing what you love. And let's have fun doing it together!

With love xo

Yvette

Preface

Follow your bliss and the Universe will open doors for you where there were only walls.

Joseph Campbell

WHAT EXACTLY IS A SOULPRENEUR?

A Soulpreneur is someone who chooses to take their soul's lead in their career or business. Someone who believes in a deeper meaning for their work and reason for being on this planet at this time. You are here because you are one of them.

We are all born with a purpose. An agreement our soul made before we were born. A soul contract.

Everyone has a personal soul lesson and mission: perhaps to learn love, compassion, forgiveness or resilience.

Some, like you and me, are also here with a global mission. Whether it be within your existing professional career, or a new business you are guided to create, a book you are guided to write, or an album you feel called to create. Or whether it be a philanthropic path, where your soul is called—inexplicably—to rise up and speak up for charities or causes. To be a voice for the voiceless.

This book is here to guide and support you. To give you clarity on your next steps, confidence to take action and an understanding of how to stand up, be seen, be heard and shine in your own unique way. Even as a sensitive soul. **Especially** as a sensitive soul.

We're seeing more and more Soulpreneurs stepping up. The rise of the Soulpreneur is happening. It's time.

The digital age has created opportunities to reach more souls than ever before. We've been blessed with this opportunity to radiate our love and light to millions across the world in an instant. This digital world is moving at lightning speed. We must embrace it to grow our careers and communities, while continuing to deepen our connection and honour our roots through traditional methods like books, art, events and purposeful products.

So, who are we as Soulpreneurs?

We are a global community of aspiring authors, artists, speakers, creatives, coaches, bloggers, musicians, healers, activists and all sorts of lightworkers in various forms. From natural beauty businesses to soulful jewellery designers, and professionals from virtual assistants to lawyers and bookkeepers. From the creative or healing arts, to the culinary or martial arts!

The vocation is irrelevant. The intention is everything. We are the ones leading with love. We lead with kindness. We lead by example.

- *We are a diverse bunch with a common desire to come together to share our story, our message, our gifts, and to bring more love, light, connection and joy to the world without burning ourselves out.*
- *We want to start and grow profitable careers and businesses, while diving deep into our soul calling, our work in the world and our audience.*

- *We are ready to dissolve the outdated belief that we are not allowed to earn good money for healing or creative work.*
- *We give ourselves permission to desire and receive prosperity.*
- *We believe that authenticity attracts abundance and that living our truth is the ticket to true happiness.*
- *We are about quality over quantity.*
- *We encourage collaboration instead of comparison. And community instead of competition.*
- *We run our careers with integrity.*
- *We are devoted to a better world.*

Sometimes Soulpreneurs may shy away from the spotlight, resisting the stage or digital space. Yet, we need to remember this isn't about us. It's about the people and the planet, who need our work. It's our responsibility to get up, show up and be the light.

- *We have the advantage of deep sensitivity and empathy with those who need us.*
- *We feel their challenges, their highs and lows, their emotions. We know what they need and want.*
- *We help. We do our best. We do what we can.*
- *We look outside the box for answers.*
- *We work together to unlock and unleash the potential of our ideas.*
- *We are warm, nurturing, welcoming.*
- *We are all about creating a business, career and life with flow, fun and freedom. A business that feels good on the inside, not just looks good on the outside.*
- *Soulpreneurs focus on spiritual and personal development as well as business and work. We nurture new friends as well as industry connections.*
- *We're about taking all this to the next level.*

As Soulpreneurs, we honour these commitments to ourselves and each other:

1. **We believe in community.** We are stronger together. We support and respect our fellow Soulpreneurs of all religions, race, gender, sexuality or socio-economic status.
2. **We embrace collaboration.** We believe in working together for the greater good. There is more than enough for all of us. No need for competition or comparison.
3. **We communicate kindly.** We know our contribution is always valued and appreciated. We are mindful and respectful with our words.
4. **We do our best.** Always. We are honest with ourselves when it's time to rest, and when it's time to rise. No need for burnout.
5. **We keep an open channel.** We honour our body, mind and soul to keep our channel clear to receive guidance from our highest power. Health over hustle.
6. **We are always authentic.** We are real with ourselves and others about who we are and what we contribute to the world.
7. **We are courageous and resilient.** We are braver and stronger than we can possibly imagine. We celebrate the highs, learn from the lows, and are prepared to bounce back brighter than ever.
8. **We are responsible for our energy.** We accept responsibility for the energy we bring to our work, community and the world. We are the light.

Because it's time to do things differently.

Preface

REDEFINING SUCCESS

The old belief that bigger is better no longer applies. It's time to redefine **success** on our own terms.

Outward success isn't a guaranteed ticket to inner fulfilment. We have woken up to the highlight reels of social media, empty promises of happiness in climbing the corporate ladder, and the stress of pushing and hustling our way through the rat race. That's why Soulpreneurship is about creating a career and life that feels good on the inside, not just looks good on the outside.

We've decided we would rather lead slow, steady, sustainable and soulful lives. A perfect alchemy of patience and persistence. Knowing that progress is progress, no matter how small the steps.

Success for us is service to others; making a positive contribution. Finding and following what lights us up and makes us feel alive:

> *It's being a positive influence in the world around us.*
> *It's having a spiritual practice and honouring our self-care.*
> *It's entrepreneurship with heart and soul.*

HOW TO USE THIS BOOK

You have an awesome opportunity to learn a lot in the coming months, as you read and action everything in this book. So, first things first. Set yourself up for Soulpreneur success. Take out your planner or calendar, grab a pen and journal, and let's get started.

Create a plan

To get the most from this book, carve out a couple of hours per chapter to apply what you learn, and write and explore the answers to questions you'll be asked along the way. Whether you work through one chapter a week, or the entire book in one full immersive weekend away, please decide now how you will action what you discover through your **Soulpreneur steps**.

You can download free and easy worksheets for each chapter at: www.yvetteluciano.com/bookclub

Commit to it

Whatever your plan is, schedule it and stick to it. Commit to actioning the exercises and work in this book, and the awesome bonus resources available to you.

Connect with other Soulpreneurs

Genuine relationships with your peers and industry are your number one asset—far more than fancy logos or websites. Soulpreneurs are big believers in community over competition, and collaboration over comparison. Our study club is ready and waiting for you at: www.yvetteluciano.com/bookclub

Chances are many of your new friends and future collaborators are waiting in the wings. Possibly even your biggest cheerleaders—people you can turn to in the tough times.

Heads up that this work will crack you open!

There may be moments while working through this book when your fears will try to hijack you, or you'll feel overwhelmed, behind or confused. This is a great sign of significant personal and business growth. It's an evolutionary process we all go through. It's common and practically a rite of passage. Please ask for support. Connect with us. We're here for you.

Schedule in self-care

Self-care is the foundation of soulful, sustainable success. This is why your daily spiritual practice and self-care time is a non-negotiable part of the journey into the soul of your work.

Start with twenty minutes of daily sacred time in the mornings, to prevent outside distractions, excuses, procrastination and other people's agendas. This twenty minutes of sacred time each day is **your** time to set up the day with clarity and confidence. Before all the emails, social media and kids' lunches, your morning sacred time is your time to connect to your soul, your spirit. It is the GPS that will guide you to create the authentic and abundant career that you deserve.

You can use this twenty minutes to meditate, listen to some peaceful music, journal, play with oracle cards, do some colouring in, whatever your soul calls for. I've created meditation gifts for you to enjoy here: www.yvetteluciano.com/bookclub

Set up your space

Setting up your sacred space will support your journey too. Your office, guest room or a dedicated corner of your lounge room is perfect. Set up an altar with all your favourite items: crystals, candles, oils, quotes, photos and a vision board. (More on how to create a vision board later in the book.) Not only will this be your go-to place for your twenty minutes of sacred time, but you can also do all of your Soulpreneur study there. In your sacred space you will have privacy, feel safe and most connected to your soul.

Alternatively, you may be best doing all of this outside in nature or in a favourite cosy nook in your local library. Where do you feel most inspired? You know where is best for you. It doesn't need to be fancy or flashy, just somewhere your soul can softly slump into as she whispers, 'ah, home.'

Look after yourself

Another Soulpreneur recommendation is to eat high-vibration foods and increase your exercise. This will help you more than you can imagine. Just minimising any chemical or processed foods and drinks will make a world of difference. When we clean up our digestive system, we can 'hear' our intuition in our gut louder and clearer than ever!

Personally, I find that the better I eat, the better the ideas come to me. And the very best ideas and solutions tend to come when I'm out exercising in nature or towards the end of a yoga session. I'm sure you know what I mean!

Nutrition and nourishment will support you. I love to eat a mostly plant-based wholefoods diet, with lots of green juices, smoothies and salads. On occasion I do enjoy indulgences, such as going to my favourite Indian restaurant with my husband or a celebratory glass of organic wine. Both good for the soul on a special occasion!

You know yourself. Get real about which foods are going to support and nourish you through this soul-stretching time.

Create a Soulpreneur soundtrack

Next up, create a Soulpreneur soundtrack. This is your go-to personal playlist to move you through moments of procrastination or fear, or for when you just need inspiration or a positive energy hit. Ideally, have one soundtrack for upbeat and motivational moments, and another soul-soothing playlist for when you're writing or creating, or making your way through the exercises.

It's easy enough to create one on Spotify or iTunes for easy access. And you're welcome to borrow mine: www.yvetteluciano.com/bookclub

Set your core intentions

Next step is to set goals and intentions for where you want to be by the end of this book. I love the concept of '3P' goals—setting intentions in the personal, professional and philanthropic categories:

> *Your* **personal** *intentions may be health, travel or relationship goals.*
> *Your* **professional** *intentions will be related to your career, business and direction as a Soulpreneur.*
> *Your* **philanthropic** *goals are driven by the people or causes who will benefit from your work.*

Set your 3P intentions now, write them down and put them somewhere you see every day: the fridge, your phone background, your desk or bathroom mirror.

~ SOULPRENEUR SUCCESS SUMMARY ~

✓ *Schedule and stick to your 'study' time.*

✓ *Schedule your daily twenty minutes of sacred time and set up a space for it.*

✓ *Clean out any low-vibration foods from your kitchen and diet.*

✓ *Start exercising regularly, if you don't already.*

✓ *Create your personal Soulpreneur soundtrack.*

✓ *Set your 3P intentions.*

Remember the pace for working through this book is entirely your choice. Decide what's best for you, and be devoted to making it happen. Slow, sustainable and soulful growth is much better than a speedy but sporadic approach.

Take your time. Soak it up, and enjoy diving deep into the soul of your business. She is sighing with relief at this opportunity to fully connect with you. At last.

Let's begin!

Some of the most wonderful people are
the ones who don't fit into boxes.

– Tori Amos

Introduction

I figure we'd better start at the beginning with a little background on my Soulpreneur journey and what brought me here to this moment where I'm writing the *Soulpreneurs* book for you. How did I have the great blessing and fortune to start working with the lightworking leaders of our generation?

I used to think I woke up to the work my soul is here to do one fateful day in 2010, when I was told 'you have cancer.' Recently though, I've realised that my journey as a Soulpreneur began long before that.

Back in the 1990s, I was a grunge-obsessed teenager, who discovered her first 'calling' one night watching a music-video marathon of female-fronted rock bands. I was fixated, and so lit up by all the passion, expression, creativity and realness of these rocking women. Music ignited a super power within me. It still does. Until that moment, I'd had no idea what I wanted to do with my life.

On a completely different page, I'd always loved being around children and enjoyed work experience at preschools, but I wasn't keen on the years of university required to go down that road. I was already devising a plan on how to get out of high school early!

School and I were not a good fit. I loathed it. My free spirit was in deep suffering, feeling stuck and squashed. I was terrible at sports and science and even worse at maths. My eyes went fuzzy as I glazed over numbers and times tables, as I felt overwhelmed with fear and the frustration of why I just couldn't 'get it.'

I became restless and rebellious and couldn't sit still in class. The only subject I ever flourished in was an elective in high school called *Society and Culture,* when the only teacher I ever connected with let me do a project on the Australian music subculture. From memory, it's the only time I received top marks.

Always in trouble for talking in class, 'using school as a social activity,' questioning the relevance of what we were learning, never doing my homework and turning up late (and most days not at all). Even the priest who led our fortnightly bible studies called my mother to express his concern about my questioning God's gender!

Getting suspended several times and eventually almost expelled from a respected high school in an affluent area of North Shore Sydney meant that this wasn't the easiest time for my parents, but it felt like a blessing to me. With my angst-filled teenage mind, I would write dark poetry and stories all asking the same question: *When are they finally going to let me be free?*

My relationship with rules has never been a good one. My wild soul shudders at 'the system.' My skin crawls at being told to do things a certain way 'just because.' I developed a disdain and disrespect for authority. I was your typical rebel without a cause. A total bad-ass in combat boots and charcoal eyeliner. And I was becoming more theatrical every day. I should have majored in drama!

I kept finding more and more ways to draw negative attention to myself, to find a way to leave school and get out of a system that I felt dysfunctional in. I understand now that the school system at that time was simply out of alignment with my soul. I understand now that, as an Indigo, it wasn't part of my soul's blueprint. I wanted to grow up quickly and get out into the world.

Eventually, I wore my parents down. When I was sixteen, they let me leave school to start a hairdressing apprenticeship. In a blaze of glory, I burned my schoolbooks and ran away from the school system as fast as I could. And I never looked back. My life began that day.

With my bass guitar in one hand and my best friend Emmie in the other, we started out first band Venusbelle in the late nineties, mostly covering our favourite songs by Hole, L7, Veruca Salt and my favourite Australian band Magic Dirt. I'll admit we weren't very good at that early stage, although I'm proud that we just got out there and simply started before we were ready. Sneaking into other band's shows and navigating our way to our own gigs, we just **got started**!

Over time (and many different drummers) our playing improved, as did our songs. We started to find our way. I became the self-appointed band manager, which led to helping my friends' bands just for fun, free tickets and drinks from their rider.

The best part was that through sheer passion, enthusiasm and dedication, I landed a dream job in Australia's leading music studio. That dream day job paid for band rehearsal spaces, bass strings, an abundance of charcoal eyeliner, and the rent on my inner-city pad, which hosted many afterparties and smelly out-of-town musos on my lounge room floor.

By the time I turned twenty, I had fully immersed myself in the music world. My soul finally felt wild and free.

At first I thought the best thing was spending day in and day out with my favourite bands, with free tickets and recording time for my band. However, along the way I developed lifelong relationships with the record label staffers, who loved my wide-eyed enthusiasm about the industry. The fact was I just wanted to help everyone. I always knew that a rising tide lifts all ships.

Music didn't just change my life. It saved it. I needed to give something back to this magical world. I know the power that one song can have on a teenager in their darkest hour, or an adult in a moment of need. I know that every song has a soul, and that song has **chosen** its artist to deliver it to those who need to hear its message. That was my drive, my **why**.

I was never afraid to ask questions about the latest music industry trends or marketing practices. How do we get these artists and these songs out there? The music industry execs were so generous and happy to share everything they knew. Studio days are long. This was before the days of the smartphone, so there were endless hours of real connection and conversation during those studio days.

I became obsessed with learning how the mysterious music industry worked, implementing all that I was learning for my own and my friends' bands, putting it all into practice and getting our songs out there. My curiosity and passion eventually led me to a full-time role at the largest record company in the world—Sony Music.

2005 was a great year for me all round, because that's when I met the love of my life, Isac. An incredible artist and musician, I met him playing in a band together. Of course. We moved in together almost instantly, though we were passing ships in the night. He toured the country and travelled with his band internationally, while I spent most of my waking moments in the

Sony office, or backstage at a concert or radio station. Excitedly working my way from the ground up, I rose through promotions and publicity to marketing, then into my dream position in artist management, touring and events. I worked hard. I partied hard.

Then, after five years at the legendary record company, the Universe decided to change my direction. I was diagnosed with cancer, after discovering an almond-like lump in my breast while on honeymoon with Isac. During the last weeks of my twenties, my life completely changed course. Or did it?

I was out of the music industry for a year, during which time I devoted myself to healing and discovered a whole other life. A polar opposite life filled with green juice, yoga, meditation, angel cards and affirmations, which I balanced with the latest modern medicine, including chemotherapy and radiation. I lost my hair, I lost a breast, but I gained a connection with my soul and an inner strength that I wouldn't trade for anything.

By the time I received the all clear from my medical team, I felt called to a different direction from the music biz: into health coaching and yoga teaching!

Six months into my new life, I discovered that, instead of simply focusing on my own coaching career, I loved helping my fellow health practitioner friends lift their profiles and platforms, in a similar way to helping other bands ten years earlier. Helping others shine in the spotlight felt more fulfilling than being in the spotlight myself.

Before I could blink, I was earning an income from managing the PR and marketing for some of the biggest bloggers in the wellbeing world. Next blink, I noticed a lack of professional and purpose-driven events and speaking opportunities for them. Earth Events was born.

Since then, I've had the pleasure of working with many of my favourite teachers, including the team at Food Matters, Gabby Bernstein, Pete Evans, Gala Darling and Wes Carr (who I'd first worked with in the music biz ten years earlier). But my very first blogging client was the late, great Jess Ainscough who, after years of working together, became a huge cheerleader for me to extend my work in the world.

Jess passing away was a catalyst for the deepest and darkest soul-searching year of my life. Then it was time for yet another career redirection.

After all my years of working with these rock stars and record companies, celebrity chefs and New York Times bestselling authors, I felt a deep call to create an opportunity for the new wave of lightworkers and leaders. This is how the Soulpreneurs course, events and masterminds began and spread all over Australia and the world—my opportunity to help the up-and-comers. I fell so deeply in love with the work I was doing in the Soulpreneurs arm of my business that I decided to devote myself almost entirely to it.

Honestly, it was terrifying to let go of Earth Events and the marketing and PR agency because, on the surface, I had everything that most entrepreneurs seek: a great team, beautiful office, impressive clients and financial abundance beyond my wildest dreams. However, a part of me wasn't fulfilled. After four years of Earth Events, I realised that working on the high-profile, high-pressure tours and campaigns was no longer aligned with my soul.

At the same time, I kept meeting these little-known healers, writers and creatives who I believed in deeply. I felt sad and frustrated seeing them struggle to break into their industry or build an audience. That's why it made so much more sense to focus on Soulpreneurs. Yes, I was proud of the work I'd completed with incredible leaders, but it was time for me to refocus on raising the new wave, the Soulpreneurs.

It pulled at me, it called to me, and my soul wouldn't let me shake off the calling. Even though my ego was terrified of 'giving up' the fortunes and famous clients. *Oh ego, do you see us now? I told you that you had nothing to worry about.*

You see, the ego is your ultimate manipulator and mind trickster. My ego loves to show up as Her Highness, Queen Resistance. Every time I've experienced significant growth in my business and life, it was always preceded by resistance.

I will certainly go deeper into this later in the book, because if I didn't have my own rituals, thanks to healers and coaches who helped me through those times, I wouldn't be here writing this book now. Earth Events wouldn't have happened. I'd never have worked with the leaders of the mind-body-spirit industry. I would never have started my first band or landed my dream job in the music industry.

However, the reality is that growth isn't always a shiny inspiration quote on Instagram. It can be a difficult and dark process, and we question everything about ourselves, our dreams and our purpose. That's why I'm committed to supporting you on this path. That's why Soulpreneurs was born. First as a course and coaching. Then as events and masterminds.

And now, this book! The pages that you're holding in your hands.

Just like the course and events, this *Soulpreneurs* book covers almost everything you could possibly need to know in your first years of business. This book is your stepping stone to shining as brightly as the Soulpreneur you are here on this planet to be. My dream is that you can stop signing up for an overload of enewsletters, books and courses. Let's get you out of overwhelm and into action.

Here's what you can expect from the coming chapters:

- Get clear on your true purpose and clarify any confusion.
- Set up a soulful and sustainable approach to your career (no burnout!)
- Reignite the fun and play that has been missing in your workdays.
- Redefine your measurements of success.
- Have courage to move forward, dissolve old blocks and understand your true worth and potential.
- Understand pricing and step into your prosperity, so you can make money and make a difference.
- Clarify your beautiful business and branding.
- Connect with your audience.
- Build your digital platforms, from your website to your social media channels and email list.
- Share your message through both your own digital platforms and media, as well as TV and traditional platforms.
- Take your next steps in your speaking or writing career. Become a magnet for book deals and speaking gigs!

And all with a straightforward yet soulful approach that speaks your language. So, now that you know a little more about my path to Soulpreneurship, let's start yours.

part ONE

Clarity

chapter ONE

The Real Reason You Are Here

> I've always loved butterflies, because they remind us that it's never too late to transform ourselves.
>
> – Drew Barrymore

Soulpreneurs do things differently. We step out of the safety of the status quo, to uncover what we are really here to do. This is rarely an easy journey or clear path, as we have a lifetime of baggage and blocks. Stories we have been told, stories we have told ourselves and instructions we have been told to follow, in order to live a life that fits in with our society and culture.

Our well-meaning family and friends wanted to protect us. Our school teachers tried to fit us into a structure, reshaping and remodelling us from a circle to a square. The media, corporations and government felt safer when we played small, bought into, thought and lived in line with what we were told. Many of us have been told to 'be realistic,' to have a plan B (or C or D).

Over the years, that message has created confusion within ourselves about who we really are. The lines have become blurry and we have lost ourselves ... almost. And yet, it's never too late. It's better to be a wolf for a day than a sheep for a lifetime. Our wolf instincts never die. That part of us is still within.

In these first chapters, we start to uncover your true self again—your true voice and your clear purpose. Later chapters will ignite your courage and light up the steps to bring your dream to life.

We start with self-enquiry, because **you** are the foundation of it all. You need to wade through the tides and times that have gone before, to open and realise your true dreams and desires. Self-enquiry helps you create that feel-good career. The one that doesn't just look good on the outside, but fits perfectly and fulfils you.

Whether you're fresh to this kind of learning, or have been a personal development junkie for years, let's do this check-in now, before the rest of the lessons unfold over the coming chapters.

Some of what you discover may be familiar. Other discoveries could be brand new. Keep an open mind. We grow and evolve so quickly at times, so we never completely finish or master our personal self-enquiry.

Many of us have been quashing our soul's voice for years. Trying to fit in, afraid to stand out, drinking too much, numbing with drugs, seeking approval, following friends, parents or partners, sizing up our lives by what we see on TV and in magazines, comparing ourselves on social media.

We live in a society where it feels safer to follow the crowd and fit in. Our soul has been beaten down and ignored, so it takes time to allow her to come through fully. To be seen, to be heard. We are so darn confused about what we are here to do, because we have no idea who we are, who we truly are. But do you think your soul fits in a perfect little box? No! Your soul doesn't colour within the lines.

The soul of your business has been waiting for the opportunity to take centre stage. Now she wants you to step into your spotlight. Be seen, heard and expressed. Fully.

So, let's take the time to get to know her. Let's take the time to get to know **you**. Even if you've done some of these exercises before, please follow the steps and do them again. Why? Because what you discovered about yourself last year, last month or last week may already have evolved. There may be more that's now ready to be revealed, or you may have outgrown what you thought you knew. This is why we do self-enquiry over again.

You will only get out of this book what you put in, so keep showing up and believing there is more to uncover. It's a lifelong journey to undo the soul-quashing patterns from our past. But you have plenty of time.

> They tried to bury us.
> They didn't know we were seeds.
> – Dinos Christianopoulos

TRUTH TRIFECTA: **TALENTS, VALUES, INTENTIONS**

The first step to finding clarity around your life as a Soulpreneur is to reflect on what brought you here:

> *Why are you on this planet at this exact moment in time?*
> *Why did you pick up this book?*
> *Why did Soulpreneurs catch your eye?*

There is a passion, a calling, and a light within you that led you to this moment. You want to create meaningful success that is not only fulfilling, but also in true alignment with why you are here. Your truth.

To do this, let's start by exploring your Truth Trifecta. Your Truth Trifecta is when you integrate your talents, values and intentions. These are distinct aspects, each one of them guiding you to ensure you are on the right path.

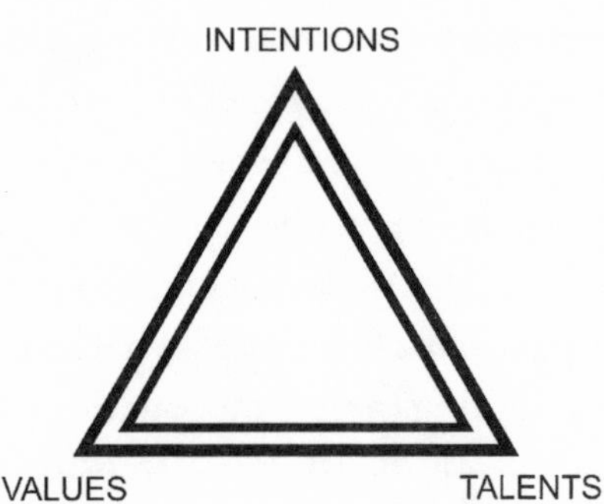

Your **talents** are what you're good at, such as writing, cooking, teaching, speaking, listening, creating, organising, technology, research, making people laugh or taking care of them.

Your **values** are what you care about, which could be health, freedom, expression, community, peace, philathropy, compassion, beauty, independence or self-love.

And the **intentions** of your work are about the end result you hope to reach, which may include helping people get fit or well, moving people to dance or sing, inspiring others with your story or simply creating experiences or products that make people feel good.

Now, a quick word before we start exploring your purpose. While you may be one of those driven people who has always known what you want to do with your life, most people on the path to Soulpreneurship find themselves here after years of work in other fields. Admin, sales, marketing, waitressing, whatever it is. After exploring your purpose here, you may feel excited to dive straight in and quit your day job, leaving behind your past skills, experience and pay cheque, to launch straight into full-time creating, coaching or healing. It's the dream picture that many online entrepreneurs are painting.

However before you do, please remember: **soulful, steady, sustainable businesses take time**. While we all want to be out there serving the world as quickly as we can, which is admirable, do give yourself the peace and patience to take it slow and steady. Be the tortoise, not the hare.

You can still share your light through every moment of every day. Give your day job customers extra love and light. Be grateful for your employer who pays you each month. Smile at strangers and do little acts of kindness on the commute to work in the morning. Volunteer in the evenings or weekends—even better if it's in line with the vocation you're moving towards! These are all beautiful ways of sharing your soul and light.

YOUR TALENTS

When I was called into healing work through my cancer diagnosis, I found myself so determined and obsessed with the next evolution of my Soulpreneur path that I pushed aside my ten plus years in media and marketing. I thought that the only way to heal the world was to become a health coach or yoga teacher. So I ventured down that path.

I learnt so much and I loved coaching. Along the way, I became friends with many other life and health coaches who I adored. Interestingly, I noticed my natural talents and instinct kicking in to help them with their marketing. Almost instantly, I noticed how much it was lighting me up to see my fellow coaches succeed.

I found myself giving advice to my own healers about their marketing. I couldn't help myself! It was the same pattern and calling that I'd felt back in my music days.

When I see natural-born creatives or healers hindered by their lack of marketing or business knowledge, I feel frustrated. Most of them have spent years and years mastering their craft, but have little idea how to actually make a living from their gifts. They get lost trying to get a quality logo or website made, let alone using social media or getting media coverage. They struggle to find enough paying clients or audience members to pay the bills. They lose their fire and their confidence is extinguished.

This is a passion point within my soul. It fires me up. While I was a great health coach, I'm an even better marketer, and a natural-born promoter and publicist.

Let's be honest with ourselves about our innate talents. Build your confidence by taking stock of your existing skills and experience. Many lightworkers help the world through 'regular' jobs. Creatives and healers come in all shapes, sizes and vocations. So, let's tap into your talents.

SOULPRENEUR STEPS

List all of the skills and experience you already have that could be redirected into more soul-fulfilling work. Ideas include:

Ability to make friends easily
Accounting/money management
Art
Attention to detail
Baking
Caring for people
Ceramics
Communicating
Connection and networking
Cooking
Decision-making
Editing
Fitness

Gardening
Great with animals or children
Graphic design
High energy
Hosting or creating experiences
Intuition
Inventing
Juggling
Languages
Leading
Listening
Making people laugh
Marketing
Massage
Mechanical abilities
Meditating
Motivating others
Music
Negotiating
Nurturing others
Organising
People skills
Photography
Planning
Problem-solving
Programming
Project management
Promoting
Raising money
Reading
Research
Sensitivity
Sewing
Sign language
Singing
Social networking
Soothing or supporting people
Storytelling
Teaching or training
Tech whiz
Typing
Video creation
Visualising
Woodwork
Writing
Yoga

....

....

....

....

YOUR VALUES

The foundation of a soulfully-aligned career is working within our values. This is the one element that is non-negotiable for Soulpreneurs. We can't bear the feeling that we are 'selling out' on what is true to our soul, true to the core of who we are.

While it's important that we stay open-minded and not become too idealistic (I can be guilty of this), it's imperative that we have a deep awareness of our values. These values will be magnetic to clients, customers, partners and an audience, as we organically tend to attract people with the same values.

SOULPRENEUR STEPS

Look at the list below and decide what you want people to say about you. If they were asked to define you and your work in the world in three words, what would they say you stand for? Feel free to add your own.

Accountability
Accessibility
Affordability
Altruism
Beauty
Belonging
Benevolence
Boldness
Bravery
Charity
Cleanliness
Commitment
Compassion
Courage
Consciousness
Consistency
Connection
Contribution
Collaboration
Creativity
Credibility
Daring
Depth
Devotion
Diplomacy
Discernment
Discovery
Dreaming
Drive
Dynamism
Education
Effectiveness
Elegance
Empathy
Endurance
Energy
Enjoyment
Enlightenment
Entertainment
Excellence
Excitement
Experience
Expertise
Expressiveness
Evolution

Fairness
Faith
Fame
Family
Fashion
Fierceness
Fitness
Flexibility
Flow
Focus
Freedom
Friendliness
Fun
Generosity
Gentleness
Genuineness
Grace
Guidance
Happiness
Harmony
Health
Honesty
Hope
Hospitality
Humility
Humour
Imagination
Impact
Independence
Insight
Inspiration
Integrity
Intelligence
Intimacy
Intuition
Inventiveness
Joy
Justice
Kindness
Knowledge
Lavishness
Leadership
Learning
Liberation
Liberty
Logic
Longevity
Love
Loyalty
Majesty
Making a difference
Mastery
Maturity
Mindfulness
Moderation
Modesty
Motivation
Mysteriousness
Open-mindedness
Optimism
Originality
Passion
Peace
Perfection
Perseverance
Persistence
Philanthropy
Play
Pleasure
Popularity
Practicality
Pragmatism
Precision
Presence
Privacy
Proactivity
Professionalism
Prosperity
Purity
Qualification
Realism
Refinement
Relaxation
Reliability
Resilience
Revolution
Respect
Sacredness
Security
Self-control
Selflessness
Self-love
Self-sufficiency
Serenity
Service
Significance
Speed
Uniqueness
Wellness

YOUR INTENTIONS

Here's the biggie! What is the intention of your work in the world? What is the final result or contribution you wish to make? This intention or 'why' will drive you.

When I wake up in the morning, before I've even opened my eyes, I'm already thinking about work. Yes, this is borderline workaholism, although it truly doesn't feel like work to me. It feels like a belly full of creative butterflies.

Almost every day, I'm excited by the opportunity to have another whole day on this planet to create something that serves the world, to bring it to life with people I love, and to be of service. So while, yes, I may be a workaholic, this work is an expression of my soul. My passion. This obsession is nothing new for me. This passion and excitement is very similar to the passion that I once had for my band in my teens and my record company artists in my twenties.

Moderation, balance and boundaries are still areas I'm working on! Some may say there are a few too little boundaries for me between work and play, friends and clients, business and spirituality. This is something that will definitely be a higher priority when I have children. For now, I just feel so fortunate to be completely in love with what I do.

And you deserve that too. You deserve a career you love to wake up to. You deserve a life that is free from snooze-button mornings and soul-quashing meetings.

This doesn't mean that I love 100% of my business responsibilities. Meetings with my accountant—bless her—are certainly not the highlight of my day. And I'm yet to hear of someone who loves 100% of their workday, as no-one cruises through every day without facing challenges. There will always be aspects you're excited to wake up for. And there will always be aspects you're not. You may face difficult clients, writer's block, disagreements with business partners, venues not returning calls or critics on social media.

And when you do, it's your intentions and your 'why' that will get you through. Your purpose will make you feel excited about your work before you even open your eyes.

Back when I was working in events and PR, there were always tight deadlines, uncontrollable elements and rogue reporters to contend with. In those challenging moments, I needed to keep my passionate, heart-centred clients and creatives on track and on time.

Just like you, they were always coming up with brilliant new ideas and ways to help the world, so keeping them focused on existing projects was difficult. Distractions from shiny new objects and ideas, being emotionally hijacked by a journalist or negative comments on social media were enough to put the brakes on everything we were doing. Artists didn't always stick to plans, social media schedules or media messaging. And it was our team's job to clean up the mess … lovingly!

Your business, partners and projects won't always be easy or go to plan, which is why having a strong intention will always bring you home. It will remind you why you do what you do, and why you need to keep going.

Every day I remind myself of my intention to help the Soulpreneurs I love, and to put more money in the hands of the healers and creatives. As a deeper intention, I desire to leave the world a healthier, happier place than when I arrived, and to make a positive contribution to this planet and these people I love so much.

We dive deeper into uncovering your why and your intentions in the coming chapters. For now, please start soul scribbling: what are the intentions of your soul's work in the world?

~ SOULPRENEUR SUCCESS SUMMARY ~

✓ *Reflect on your skills and experience, then list out your talents.*

✓ *Explore what you truly care about and define what you value most.*

✓ *Decide what it is that drives you, what's your core motivation or desired outcome. Then write down your Soulpreneur intention.*

chapter TWO

Clarity, Focus, Goals

I think a spiritual journey is not so much
a journey of discovery. It's a journey of recovery.
It's a journey of uncovering your own inner nature.
It's already there.

– **Billy Corgan**

Where do you find your sense of purpose? How do you set your intentions? Your why? And how do you carry that through all you do? These are the questions we'll be exploring throughout this chapter, as you gain clarity and focus, getting specific around your goals.

CAREER VISION AND SOUL MISSION

With your Truth Trifecta underway—don't worry, it doesn't have to be perfect—it's time to get cosy with your clear career vision and deepen the understanding of your soul's mission here on Earth.

I believe that every being is born with a personal purpose and lesson. This may be to learn love, compassion, surrender, resilience, forgiveness or selflessness. We learn these soul lessons through all our life experiences. Our life experiences lead to personal and soul growth. Our soul grows by experiencing the lesson we set out to learn when we selected this body, time, parents and circumstances.

Some souls chose an easy lifetime, the kindergarten of lessons this round—either because we had big soul work last lifetime and needed a breather, or because something big is coming next time around. However, many of our souls 'signed' a pre-birth sacred contract to experience a master's degree worth of soul lessons in this lifetime! Not only are we here with a personal purpose, we are also here with a global purpose, a mission to positively impact the world in this lifetime. In a big way.

Until we accept and embody this role—the soul contract, the decision made before we were born—the Universe will continue to redirect us back towards our purpose and mission. No matter how hard we try, we will be course corrected over and over. Just like an annoying GPS. The more that we ignore the little signs and soft whispers, the louder and brighter they will become. Synchronicities are impossible to ignore. Those 'coincidences' will keep popping up.

Those inexplicable feelings of simply being called or pulled like a magnet towards something that may not make sense on paper or in your head, yet the siren song gets louder and the feeling grows deeper. If we continue to ignore the pull, the signs, the call, the Universe starts to take more dramatic and drastic actions.

One day we wake up to the trauma. Perhaps dis-ease, divorce or the death of a loved one. Then we're thrown to our knees, sobbing on the cold hard floor in the middle of the night. Those darkest of moments in our deepest weakness are the moments when we arise in our greatest strength, as we embrace the full power and spectrum of our soul.

This is when we face the crossroads. This is when we rise into our greatest self, or fall into anxiety or addictions.

I have experienced both responses and gone down both paths. Years ago, it was addiction to drugs, drink, drama and destruction that swallowed me. That temporarily distracted me from my pain, sent me on a dark downward spiral and dimmed my light.

Now I choose a new path. I choose to feel it all, and fuel my fire: my devotion to helping others. As I choose to dive deep and heal the hurt, it opens up my compassion and capacity to help others heal too. I now choose to rest and then to rise.

When I was diagnosed with cancer, I shifted my entire career to one of higher service and healing for myself and others. I course corrected from my previous career and life. When my best friend passed away, I transformed my business to one of deeper soul fulfilment and service to my soul sisters and brothers. I course corrected again. Through my dark nights and challenges re having a baby and becoming a mother, I have become clear on the work I wish to do in the future, to support my fellow yearning mothers. Yes, I'm still course correcting.

There is a wonderful book called *Super Survivors* that flew off the shelf and into my lap in a bookstore in New York, when I was in a dark time years ago. The first page I opened up said: *We don't always bounce back, sometimes we bounce forward.* Since then, it has become one of my life's mantras.

In full transparency, I do not always live in the light. Like you, I continue to have dark days, times when I feel tempted to buy a ticket on the downward spiral. But now I feel it, I embrace it. I call in the help of a healer, or the faeries, or the beach, rather than the liquor store. And I course correct, knowing that the discomfort is a sign not to be ignored.

DON'T WAIT FOR THE DIVORCE, DIAGNOSIS OR DEATH

In Bronnie Ware's *Top Regrets of the Dying,* she shares that the number one regret on a person's deathbed is: *I wish I'd had the courage to live a life true to myself, not the life others expected of me.*

Why do we wait until these darkest hours, to get real with ourselves on who we are and what we want in our life? We waste so much time and effort seeking approval, validation or justification of our desires and dreams, explaining ourselves, hiding ourselves and being safe and 'realistic' about what is possible for us. We compromise. We hide. We shelter our real selves, our real wishes, under the covers. Then only when our minds, bodies and souls can't take it anymore and tell us through our depression, our divorce, our dis-ease that what we are doing can't continue, do we truly own who we are.

For some, that may feel too little too late, though I don't believe that's true. Even if you only had two days left on this planet, that's a whole two days to embrace and express who you really are. To leave a legacy for the people you come into contact with during those precious days. Your legacy that will be handed to the next generation. And if you're lucky enough to have more time than that, what a miracle!

How lucky you are to be waking up to this now! Everything that led you to this point had a purpose. You'll discover that when you embody your truth. What appears right now to have been random dots will connect into a big beautiful picture when you reflect back. You don't need to see that right now. It will come.

Are you stuck feeling it's too late or you're too old? I hear that a lot. It's time to shake off that excuse. We'll talk more later about the excuses and blocks that bind us. For now, allow me remind you that Louise Hay, the heavenly founder of the incredible publishing company Hay House (who got this very book into your hands), only started the company at the age of sixty! She didn't have access to nearly half the amount of resources and support you have now, with the assistance of the World Wide Web and books, courses and communities like *Soulpreneurs*.

Which leads me to repeat the question: **Why do we wait?**

One of the blessings in my life is my scans and oncologist check-ups. During these anxiety-filled days in hospital gowns, on cold and claustrophobic scanning beds, I am faced with my greatest fears. I am reminded of my mortality and the fact that I live with a dis-ease that doesn't have the most positive prognosis. Yet this is a bittersweet blessing, because it challenges me physically, emotionally and spiritually to stretch my soul and my strength.

These medical check-up days double as a powerful soul check-in, as I lie there in total vulnerability, all alone in a hospital gown, just me and the machines in total isolation. Even the scanning technicians are behind radiation-proof walls and windows. And I'm reminded that one day, like all of us, I will leave this planet as I arrived ... completely on my own.

How do I want to feel when that day comes? Who do I want to know I helped? What contribution will I be proud to have made?

I remember when I was first diagnosed and facing these questions. I felt full of shame and regret that everything in my life up until that point had felt so self-indulgent. That I had made no positive contribution and that my existence on this planet had been one of taking, not giving.

My existence didn't feel balanced. I regretted that I wasn't helping animals, which I'd felt called to do since I first went vegetarian at fourteen. That my recent career highlights were all driven by ego. That my guitars were starting to rust and becoming covered in dust. That I hadn't been there for friends who needed me, because I was too busy with my glamorous life. Gosh ... I wasn't even recycling my rubbish properly!

Luckily these days, my bittersweet scan experiences are not filled with as many regrets, but just enough little ones to keep me on track. I tend to do a spring-clean of my business and life around scanning times.

While I don't wish my specific experience on anyone, what can you do to create these routine soul check-ins in your life? I don't want you to be like me. I don't want you to wait for a disease or the death of a loved one to take stock of where you are. To wake up. To look at your life with perspective.

I know that we all think life is long and we'll be around forever ... until we realise it's not and we won't. We don't realise how short and precious life is until it's almost gone.

Your life is a blessing. Your life is a miracle. In the big picture, it's irrelevant how long or short your life is. This doesn't influence the impact you can make in this world, or the pride and fulfilment you can feel the day you leave this blue planet.

Look at the short yet significant lives of Princess Diana or Jimi Hendrix! The legacy they left will continue for many lifetimes. Let's focus our lives and years on quality not quantity. Soulpreneurs can create more positive impact in one day than others might in an entire lifetime.

What can you do? Will you start today? What will your legacy be?

My legacy is that I stayed on course
from the beginning to the end, because I
believed in something inside of me.

– **Tina Turner**

SOULPRENEUR STEPS

Let's explore the following questions, to help **get clear on your soul vision** for this lifetime. Prepare to go deep! Give as much detail as possible. Use your emotions and sensitivity to connect with the questions. And remember, our darkest times can hold our deepest lessons.

Who do you most want to help or create for?

....

....

Why do you want to pursue this work?

....

....

What personal experiences and challenges relate to this calling?

....

....

What are the darkest times and lessons you have experienced in your life? (List this as a timeline from your earliest memories.)

....

....

What do people ask you for help or advice on?

....

....

How would the five people closest to you describe you?

....

....

Do you have any professional background already that relates to this intention?

....

....

What exactly do you want to do?

....

....

Which companies, personalities or creatives do you admire most and why?

....

....

Once you're done, you can use them to make a crystal clear career vision statement, starting with: 'I am ...' For example:

> *I am running my own successful business selling eco home products, which allows me to have a great work-life balance and spend my days working from home.*
>
> or
>
> *I am thriving as an artist, selling my work online and regularly taking opportunities to travel the countryside with my family to host art shows.*

Include as much or as little detail as you like, such as how your career makes you feel, how much money you're earning or how many hours a week you work. For multi-passionate Soulpreneurs who may have too many ideas, focus on your top dreams. The ones that light you up more than anything else.

....

....

....

Let's remember that through these exercises we are aiming for progress, not perfection. Every exercise you do is a small step that will make a significant difference.

Getting clear on your vision is the ticket to a peaceful and prosperous life. Your vision can and probably will keep evolving, but we need to start somewhere. So, think about the future and imagine where you want your career and life to be this time next year ... in five years ... and beyond!

STILL DON'T KNOW WHAT YOU WANT TO DO?

Whether you have no ideas or fifty of them, I believe that deep down we know our life purpose. The obstacle comes when we resist owning it. You might experience resistance because truly owning your purpose means you'll need to face your fears, step up and out into the unknown, make big sacrifices or let people finally see the true you, which is daunting.

You might also find your life purpose by looking at your passions. When looking at your passions—which could include health, fitness, yoga, food, writing, photography, travel, film, art or music—take a look at the multiple models you can explore.

A word of caution ...

Having multiple ideas may be what's holding you back, because you have an excuse to never follow through on anything. Yes, you're allowed to be multi-passionate and have several aspects to your business, career and life. Just take it one step and one project at a time!

SOULPRENEUR STEPS

Take a look at the following example, then explore your own passions in a similar way.

If you're passionate about food, related business ideas could be:

> *opening a cafe*
> *teaching cookery classes online or in-person*
> *writing a food blog*
> *becoming a food journalist*
> *developing food products*
> *running a foodie festival or markets*
> *releasing cookbooks*
> *becoming a chef or a food stylist*
> *copywriting for food businesses*
> *being a nutritionist or a private chef*
> *starting a catering company*
> *running online seminars or series with foodies*
> *creating a documentary*
> *helping your favourite foodies with their marketing or social media*

You can do this exploration in any industry. Just pick your passion, then go from there. Get real about the dreams hiding behind your fears. Dig deeper. Live out your career fantasies in your head and then on the lines below. Go wild. Pick one area you are passionate about and explore all areas of possibility in that industry.

....

....

....

Look back at the first part of your Truth Trifecta—your talents—and see how they could apply to your ideas about your purpose.

VISION AND MISSION

Trying to create success by the definitions of others is the reason I hear stories every day of so-called 'successful' entrepreneurs or creatives who reach the goal, get the corner window office, the promotion, the fame, the number one album or book ... and feel nothing. They reach the top of the mountain, only to look around and ask: Is this it?

Why do so many famous stars turn to alcohol or drugs, when they are at the top of their game? At the peak of their career?

As Jim Carrey said: *I think everybody should get rich and famous, so they can see that it's not the answer.*

Start thinking about how you define success for yourself. I'll go first, as an example. Here are my personal measurements of success in my career and business:

1. Feels connected to my soul
2. Feels connected to the soul of my community
3. Makes a positive contribution to the world
4. Makes my 14-year-old past self (and my 94-year-old future self) feel proud
5. Profitable

Maybe yours are similar. Perhaps they're completely different.

SOULPRENEUR STEPS

Explore your definition of success. List as many aspects as you like and rank them in their order of importance.

....

....

....

....

....

....

....

....

~ SOULPRENEUR SUCCESS SUMMARY ~

✓ *Explore the lessons your soul is here to learn, then write a vision statement.*

✓ *Pick a passion and brainstorm business ideas in that industry.*

✓ *Look at how your talents fit into your aligned business ideas.*

✓ *Define success for yourself.*

chapter THREE

From Day Job to Dream Life

All our dreams can come true, if we have the courage to pursue them.

– Walt Disney

Though we've been exploring your practical experience, goals, talents, skills and missions, there's nothing like going back and dreaming. Perhaps the reason this book fell into your hands was because you've long held a dream. When you thought up your core 3P intentions right at the start, perhaps what guided you in setting them was a lifestyle and a vision of serving the world in a big and dreamy way.

One particularly strong way to feel guided towards your purpose and your dreams is to think about how you want to feel—making sure that your goals and intentions align with how you want to feel.

This is similar yet different to the values exercise in the Truth Trifecta section. They are intertwined, however the difference is mostly that our values are about our work in the outside world, whereas our feelings are internal. They are personal.

When working with a team or collaborator, it's imperative that your values are aligned, yet you may desire something different when it comes to feelings.

SOULPRENEUR STEPS

Think back to the best moments of your life, the ones that felt good on the inside. How did they feel? Now think about the times or experiences where you felt most unhappy or empty. In those moments, what were you craving to feel?

Circle the feelings below that speak to you, then go through and **shortlist your top three**. Write them on a Post-It note and stick them on your computer.

When making any career or life decisions, check in with how they align to these top three feelings. Will your decision help you feel how you want to feel?

Abundant
Accepted
Accessible
Adventurous
Affectionate
Affluent
Alive
Appreciated
Attractive
Authentic
Balanced
Blessed
Bold
Brave
Bright
Brilliant
Calm
Centred
Cheerful
Clear
Comfortable
Confident
Connected
Considerate
Courageous
Creative
Curious
Daring
Delighted
Desired
Determined
Devoted
Dynamic
Easeful
Ecstatic
Elevated
Empowered
Encouraged
Energised

Enlightened
Enthusiastic
Excited
Expressive
Fabulous
Fantastical
Feminine
Focused
Fortunate
Free
Fresh
Friendly
Fulfilled
Generous
Gentle
Genuine
Glamorous
Graceful
Grateful
Grounded
Guided
Happy
Harmonious
Healthy
Held
Homey
Hopeful
Holy
Illuminated
Important
Innovative
Inquisitive
Inspired
Integrous
Interesting
Intriguing
Inspired
Joyful
Kind
Level
Liberated
Light
Limitless
Loved
Loving
Luminous
Magical
Mindful
Masculine
Natural
New
Nourished
Nurtured
Open
Optimistic
Opulent
Passionate
Peaceful
Playful
Positive
Powerful
Prosperous
Proud
Purposeful
Quiet
Ready
Refreshed
Regal
Relaxed
Reliable
Rich
Romantic
Sacred
Safe
Secure
Seen
Sensitive
Sensual
Serene
Settled
Sexy
Sincere
Spontaneous
Solid
Soulful
Spirited
Spiritual
Strong
Successful
Supported
Sweet
Tenacious
Tender

Thankful	United	Vivacious
Thrilling	Unique	Vulnerable
Touched	Useful	Warm
Treasured	Valuable	Wealthy
Understanding	Valued	Whole
Understood	Vibrant	Wholesome

To dive deeper into your core desired feelings, I recommend Danielle LaPorte's book, *The Desire Map*.

In the meantime, here are some questions to reflect on in your journal, to continue clarifying the holistic picture of your career and life:

> *How much relaxation and rest time do you need or want?*
> *What are your health and wellness goals?*
> *Which relationships do you desire to devote more love, energy and quality time to?*
> *What travel or adventures do you dream of having?*
> *What gifts or hobbies do you want to develop?*
> *What personal interests do you wish to explore?*
> *Which people, charities or organisations do you want to help?*

Gain more clarity on your professional goals and intentions, by thinking back to your childhood and teenage dreams:

> *What did you enjoy doing in your free time as a child and as a teenager?*
> *What were your career fantasies when you were four years old? (Ask your parents if you don't remember.)*
> *What did you secretly dream of becoming when you were fourteen years old?*

- *What were your favourite books, music, movies and TV characters during your teenage years?*
- *Who did you look up to and poster your room with? What did you love about them?*

....

....

....

....

....

....

Then fast forward to the present day and think about these questions:

- *How do you enjoy spending your free time and weekends?*
- *What are your secret or most crazy career fantasies now?*
- *If money wasn't a factor, how would you choose to spend your time?*
- *What do you love to do when you are on holidays?*
- *What makes you feel most alive?*
- *What makes you feel drained?*
- *What are the topics of your favourite non-fiction books?*
- *What are the last five books you bought?*
- *What are the last five Instagram profiles you followed?*
- *What do you know more about than the average person?*
- *What do you love to talk about?*
- *Now dream big. And write!*

....

....

....

....

....

....

....

....

Not sure what lessons you have to share? Here's a further fun exercise you can try out in your journal. Write your teenage self a letter full of reflective wisdom, answering the question: *If I could give life advice to my teenage self, what would it be?*

Need some inspiration? Check out a snippet of the advice Russell Brand dished out to his younger self in the 'Note to Self' segment on US TV show, *CBS This Morning*:

> *You are going to get rich and famous and travel the world, meet loads, seriously kiddo, loads of unbelievable girls and there will be moments when you enjoy it. But I know for a fact what you already suspect. None of this stuff is the answer.*
>
> *There's a thing that you're good at: making people laugh and connecting with them. That's cool. It's really cool. Look after that, it's going to look after you. But know too that not*

everyone's going to like you. That doesn't matter. The important thing is that you like you.

I want to tell you you're alright. You have everything you need already. Try to listen to that quiet voice because that's the thing you're looking for. Some people call it love, others call it connectivity and others call it God. It's there, it's always been there, and it will always be there. And if you look after it, it will look after you.

PHILANTHROPY AND GENEROSITY

As Soulpreneurs, our philanthropic intentions and actions aren't just an afterthought or small part of our business. They are part of the foundation of who we are, what we do and why we do it. They are built into our business plan from the ground up.

Even if you aren't attracting income yet, you can start planting this seed now. The great news is that it doesn't necessarily need to be about money. This isn't just about donating a percentage of profit to a charity each year. (Although if this is what you choose to do, that's wonderful too!)

Nope, philanthropy isn't just the wonderful act of generously donating money. Let's think about all the various ways your work can create a positive impact for those who need it most.

Could it be using your platform to promote certain causes and initiatives, whether it be local fundraisers or animals looking for homes? Or something you do away from the spotlight? If you're a yoga teacher, you might offer free monthly classes in disadvantaged communities. If you're a business coach, you might offer free fortnightly sessions to financially challenged start-ups, or free ebooks to those in need.

Whatever your philanthropic efforts, they don't need to be big or flashy, they just need to be something that aligns with your gifts and your values. Philanthropy isn't just focused on raising awareness of a problem. It's about empowering change through action.

However, if you do decide to be public about raising awareness along the way, I suggest being extra respectful of the sensitivity of your audience, especially when sharing posts. Give them empowered action to take if they wish and activate them to get on board and feel good contributing.

You may be surprised to find that, while there is no financial reward, philanthropy becomes the most soul-fulfilling part of your career and life. While I'm proud of my monthly donations to charities I care about, I sometimes feel that the free ebooks or support I give to women with cancer are my greatest contribution.

We all have gifts to give. What are yours?

SOULPRENEUR STEPS

Dream day visualisation

To help gain even deeper clarity on your purpose, let's look at your desired career outcome as a visual. What is the grand final vision? By visualising and exploring your 'dream day' as a Soulpreneur, you can become oh so crystal clear on the career and life that honours your soul, wellbeing and the reason you are here on the planet in this lifetime.

You may have done this visualisation many times in the past, or this may be your first time, but I encourage you to apply this to your dream day as a Soulpreneur on this occasion.

Becoming clear on the career and life that honours your soul is a pretty big intention to set. I'm sure you'll agree! So, set aside at least one hour for this exercise: thirty minutes for the visualising part, followed by thirty minutes of journalling afterwards.

You will be accessing your imagination and entering fantasy land, which is easier for some of us than others. Remember, this is a private exercise. No-one is going to see what you're visualising in your mind. There's no need to be embarrassed.

For this visualisation, either record yourself reading the script aloud or download the audio gift I have created for you at www.yvetteluciano.com/bookclub, then listen back, with your eyes closed throughout.

Set yourself up in a comfortable, quiet, private space. If you can't find a peaceful place at home, head into nature or somewhere you'll remain undisturbed. Make some tea and settle in with your journal. If you wish to diffuse or anoint yourself with essential oils during this visualisation, I recommend frankincense and/or clary sage. You may wish to carefully place a diluted drop on your third eye (in the middle of your forehead between your eyebrows, taking care to avoid getting any in your eyes).

Sit up straight in your chair with your feet flat on the floor, or on the ground with legs crossed. Close your eyes and listen to the following guided visualisation that you've either downloaded or recorded yourself:

Take deep breaths with your hands placed softly on your belly. Breathe in fully through your nose, filling your lungs, through your chest and into your belly. Once full, exhale through your mouth and nose. Keep breathing like this.

Use the breath to clear your mind as much as possible. Let go of the thoughts about today, about work, the kids, the meals, the social media. All of that can all wait. This is your time to visualise your future.

First, take a step back to the moment that you picked up the Soulpreneurs book. Feel that excitement or nervousness. What was the outcome you hoped for by reading Soulpreneurs? Now, think about the next few weeks, after you've finished reading.

Between the moments of enthusiasm and procrastination, explore why you are doing all this. Is there one reason, a particular goal or outcome that you're hoping to achieve? Are you unsure, but feel drawn to it, like it's something you want or are meant to do for a reason you don't yet know or understand?

Now, let's go further into the future. Set a time for this dream day to take place. Is it in a couple of months or further down the track?

Start to sink in. Feel yourself moving into the energy of that time. Imagine you've jumped into a time machine and woken up on your dream day. Feel it. Visualise yourself awakening. Where are you?

Imagine the beautiful bed where you're waking up, the colour and texture of the sheets, the first sights and smells. Is it in your current house or somewhere you're hoping to move to? Is it a hotel or family home?

Visualise who you're with. Are you alone with the bed all to yourself or with your loved one, a partner, puppies, cats, your kids or a baby?

Imagine what your thoughts are about the day ahead. What is happening on this dreamy day? How are you feeling about it? Are you feeling peaceful, excited, creative, expansive? Are you buzzing because the day is full of all of your favourite people and activities, kids, clients, talks, writing, projects? Are you feeling peaceful and expansive for having nothing on your calendar?

Visualise getting up out of bed and having your shower. You start thinking about the day ahead. What's on your schedule? What exercise will you do? What will you eat? How will meditation or a spiritual practice fit into your morning? How many hours will you work? All this is possible for you.

You might be about to jump on a plane to travel to a city where you'll do a sold-out talk for hundreds of people. You may host a one-on-one session for a favourite client, who experiences deep transformation and pays you abundantly. Perhaps you're out taking beautiful photos or reading in the park all day. Anything is available to you.

Bring to mind your fantasy career. Do you have a team? Are you managing people? What clients do you help or support? Where will you work? Is it in a beautiful office with your team or by yourself at home, writing and creating? It may be a balance of both. This does not need to be all or nothing.

Think about how your dream day unfolds. How much money is coming in? What are you receiving effortlessly? How much is already in the bank? When you have a figure in your mind that feels safe and accessible, double it. Feel that more expansive figure in your bank account.

Visualise what is in your hands. Have you created physical products, published a book, written digital content? Are you arranging beautiful flowers for an event, designing jewellery, or shipping your own beauty products?

Imagine who you see on this dreamy day. Who do you connect with? Peers, clients, team members? Who is emailing or calling you with an invitation? Are you being asked to hang out, complimented on what you do, invited to collaborate, hired to speak at an upcoming event, or asked to be interviewed? When these people contact you, how do you feel? Knowing? Excited? Liberated?

Know this magical day exists for you. It does exist. You are limitless. You can do anything. This dreamy day is possible. There is no need to accept anything less. This perfect day is inevitable if you believe in yourself and do the work.

Let's close off your dream day by visualising going back to sleep that evening. You're lying in bed. Maybe you're doing some journalling or kissing your loved ones goodnight. How are you feeling as you reflect on this dream day?

You write down everything you're thankful for. What is on that list? Who is on that list? What are you grateful for that happened? Feel the gratitude and drift off to sleep knowing that you just had that magical day and that the next day you'll wake up to another one.

Feel it as if it exists right now, because it does. It exists in your future. This dream day is coming for you. It already exists.

When you're ready, open your eyes then **journal about everything that came through to you.** If you're more of a visual person, you could create a vision board instead.

Once you're done, go for a walk and feel this dream day because you deserve it. It's the life you were born to live.

Vision boards

Vision boards are physical and visual reminders of our goals, so you can easily keep your dreams at the forefront of your mind and stay on track. This is especially powerful if you are a visual person. But how do you actually make one?

Step 1: **Plan**

Before you start, complete the 'Soulpreneur steps' that you've seen so far in this book to ensure you're clear on the vision you wish to bring to life.

Step 2: **Create**

Collect images that represent what you're trying to reach. For example, pictures of a tropical destination, a new home office or home with ocean views, a bestselling book or album, a bulging bank balance. You can find images online and create a digital vision board or cut pictures out of old magazines.

Scribble notes and keywords, such as your values or desired feelings across the board to inspire you.

Step 3: **Check in**

Set your vision board aside for a day or two and look back over it with fresh eyes. Does it fill you with overwhelming joy or are you playing small and safe? Your vision board is all yours. You can make it as wild as you wish. Be sure that the dreams on there are yours, not what you think should be there. Tropical holidays or fancy cars aren't for everyone.

Step 4: **Commit**

Place your vision board somewhere you can see it every day, as a reminder of all of the wonderful manifestations coming your way. Save it to your phone, place it above your office desk, above your bed, or on your bathroom mirror. Anywhere you'll see it every day.

If you're feeling protective of your vision and would rather keep it to yourself for now, you can create a private board on Pinterest by flipping the 'Secret' toggle, so that only you will see your pinned images.

Manifesting doesn't end with creating your vision board. Your job now is to ensure you look over it at least once a day and see in your mind's eye all of your wonderful dreams coming to life. Refresh your vision board whenever you feel called. Mine gets a refresh every few months, sometimes an entire overhaul if my soul has been stretched.

UNVEILING RATHER THAN FINDING

Through the various 'Soulpreneur steps' sections in these first few chapters, you may have started to notice that, instead of looking outside of yourself for answers, we are diving within. That's because all of the answers, your true purpose, has always been within you. You were born with this in your heart, in your soul.

Our work together in this chapter and the next is simply unveiling this truth. Revealing the answers from within, the light that may have been previously hidden.

Let's invite her to rise now. It's safe for her to be seen, to be heard. It's time.

~ SOULPRENEUR SUCCESS SUMMARY ~

✓ *Consider how success* **feels** *for you.*

✓ *Remember your dreams looking backwards.*

✓ *Visualise your future dream day.*

✓ *Create a vision board of that dream day.*

chapter FOUR

Going Back to the Future

You cannot connect dots looking forward,
but you can connect dots looking backwards.
– **Steve Jobs**

Reflecting back on our childhood and teenage dreams in the earlier 'Soulpreneur steps' exercises is a chance to reignite the spark we once had about our careers and lives, before the world told us what it thought was possible for us ... before we were introduced to the word 'realistic' or the concept of a plan B, C or D.

In this chapter, you will discover that none of your work or life experiences has been insignificant. Nothing was a waste. In even the most random phases, interests and situations there was a lesson. Sometimes massive, sometimes micro.

There is magic and meaning in almost everything. With enough time and space to reflect, we can start connecting the dots.

Your favourite songs from childhood, your favourite movies during your teens, your favourite characters who you adored. Like many young girls from my generation, I was obsessed with *The Baby-Sitters Club* book series by Ann M. Martin. On reflection, I loved their soul sister connection. And hey, those Stoneybrook girls were pretty entrepreneurial when you think about it. They started their business at just thirteen years of age, with all six of them running their enterprise from a tiny bedroom with a shared phone at Claudia Kishi's place. They were the original Soulpreneur poster girls!

Then there was Madonna, who was wild and expressive, a strong woman channelling so many goddesses. And songs like *Heaven Is a Place on Earth* and *Live Your Life, Be Free* by Belinda Carlisle were my favourites for years.

It wasn't all light and bright, of course. As my teenage angst years rolled in, I moved on to the loud music and art of the Riot Grrrl rock movement, and the dark mystical vibes of the classic 90s film, *The Craft*. All significant.

Then there were the random jobs. Even the short-lived and most loathed ones. The worst? Probably my short spell as a telemarketer in my late teens. And yet, cold-calling people about holiday packages helped develop my phone manner, resilience and confidence to put myself out there. Even in the most uncomfortable situation. Once again, totally significant.

Reflect back on the questions in the previous chapter and double-check if there are any significant past times that were missed. Dig into the core messages of the books, films or music you loved, always trying to find the golden thread. The seemingly insignificant dots that weave together the bigger picture of who you are and what you're here to do.

When I first switched my career from entertainment to wellness, I sobbed because I felt all my hard work in the music industry was a waste. It was all for nothing, so I thought. I was going to have to start all over from scratch in a brand new industry.

I know now that every single moment was a dot on the bigger connect-the-dots picture of my life, and that everything in my previous career created a foundation for my future work. Music marketing principles transferred across all industries, creating influential platforms and engaged audiences. Even the seemingly insignificant jobs before the music industry (yep, even that icky cold-call telemarketing) were a foundation for my PR calls to magazine editors or Earth Events calls to potential speakers and clients.

Trust the magic in the meaning of all the moments of your life. Follow the crumbs, connect the dots, weave the thread. Trust the higher purpose. Even if it doesn't make sense to you right now.

Everything you have done, and will do, forms the foundation of extra experience, expertise, skill and talent for your soul's purpose. We're not born as naturally 'good' or 'bad' business builders. We are created through the layers. And the layers aren't just the successes or the joys or the achievements. There are extra thick and luscious layers of lessons from failures, flops and jobs we disliked or flunked. The lessons ... oh the lessons!

Money mindset maven Denise Duffield-Thomas spoke at our very first Soulpreneurs event (at the beginning, when people didn't have a clue what the word 'Soulpreneur' meant when I said it). She reassured the audience that it was totally okay for your first business to be a 'practice business' and that some of us have a couple of goes before we find and create The One.

If you have previously had a business or launched a project that didn't go as well as you'd hoped, remember you learnt more than you can imagine and it was a significant dot.

SOULPRENEUR STEPS

Grab your journal or write below, to **reflect on your dots**, going back as far as you can remember:

> *What were your favourite movies, music and books—and why?*
> *Who were your childhood heroes—and why?*
> *What are all the significant career moments of your connect-a-dot?*
> *What are the most significant experiences in your career or life (the breakdowns, the breakthroughs, the successes, the failures)?*

....

....

....

....

....

....

....

....

~ SOULPRENEUR SUCCESS SUMMARY ~

✓ *Go back through your life and note the experiences that were significant.*

✓ *Draw themes between the lessons of various times in your life.*

✓ *Identify the common threads between your interests as a child and now.*

chapter FIVE

Be Your Own Business Guru

I am my own experiment. I am my own work of art.
– **Madonna**

We are living in a time where there is an abundance of resources available to assist you on your new career or business path. Courses, coaches, teachers and resources fill our wonderful World Wide Web. We are one click away from answering almost any questions or seeking any how-to info.

While we are blessed to access this information, overwhelm and information overload can be conflicting and confusing. Which leads us to stepping further and further away from our inner truth and being our own wisest business guru. The one who has been with you all along. The one who has been planning for this your entire life, with the soul contract in hand from the start.

In this chapter, I challenge you to allow your inner wisdom, guru and guide to rise. Let her rise to centre stage and step into the spotlight for all your career decisions and business meetings.

She is the soul of your business. Ancient and wise. Much higher and holier than anything we can look up on Google. Without ego and only here to serve.

Pause here and breathe. Slow down and connect in with the soul of your business. She has been waiting your whole life for this.

The first step in this challenge is to connect deeply with your own soul, the essence of who you really are. Self-care plays a big part in this as a necessary entry point. So let's start exploring how we can take better care of **you**, and start welcoming in your beloved partner—the soul of your business.

CYCLES OF THE SOUL

Seasons

In the foodie world, we have seen a return to our roots of eating seasonally. Cooling smoothies and salads in summer, warming soups and curries in winter. It's time to honour our seasonal energy, needs and instincts in our career too.

In the past, I used to push through the year trying to go at the same consistent pace. This is the Monday to Friday corporate culture of the Western world. It's how we land in exhaustion, burnout, adrenal fatigue and depletion. We become resentful towards our business and work. It feels relentless and repetitive.

When you have the opportunity as a Soulpreneur to choose your days, hours and schedule, you can explore a better way to forward plan your year, using the guide below:

Spring: Rebirth, launching and birthing new projects and products, blossom, new life, excitement

Summer: Activity, celebration, socialising, goal-setting, seeing the full potential of dreams

Autumn: Reflection and reassessment on what stays and what goes, contemplation, shedding, change
Winter: Hibernation, going inward, creative cave and self-care cocoon

There are some exceptions. For instance, I have produced some of our most successful tours mid-winter—a time when people have more space in their social calendars. And there are some summers when I just want to rest, reflect and be with family.

Decide what is right for you and be mindful that the seasons of **your** soul won't always reflect the weather. You may go through a personal crisis during the summer, which requires you to take a winter within, and have some hibernation time. In winter, you may feel the urge to host workshops or retreats, such as the one Soulpreneurs enjoyed in Byron Bay. It was a gentle and honoured time of the year for us, diving deep into our feminine and softening to receive our soul's voice, in contrast to our high-energy Soulpreneur Summer Schools that are big on brainstorming, goals and plans.

Give yourself permission to honour the seasons of your soul. Go slow when needed. Speed up when called.

Everything in nature works to cycles. Why would we be any different? We may experience months of extroverted openness focused on the outside world, followed by months of introverted solitude and privacy. Are you at a point in your seasonal cycle of slowing down or speeding up?

Soulpreneurs must honour the cycle of serving themselves and serving others. There needs to be a beautiful balance. The better care we take of ourselves, the better care we can take of others.

Menstrual

The seasons are only one part of this conversation. There is a rise in the divine feminine leadership world, where menstrual cycles are honoured by female CEOs in planning their month. When to write, when to launch, when to rest. They advocate finding more flow in the way we lead our week, our month and our year.

Claire Baker, author of *Love Your Cycle,* believes that women's menstrual cycles are a gift, not a burden. Claire teaches that honouring the natural cycle and inner seasons helps us understand that we are four different women in every month: from smashing to-do lists one week, to feeling creative and inspired the next, then needing to withdraw and hibernate.

Understanding your menstrual magic will help you find your flow, while understanding other women in your life and work. We need to support each other in opening up these conversations and honouring where we are.

Moon

One of nature's cycles that is impossible to ignore is the moon. The lunar cycle refers to the moon's continuous orbit around the earth every 28 days. The moon can greatly influence our moods, with extreme emotional sensitivity around the full moon and much more balance, clarity and calm with the new moon.

The four main moon phases to start honouring:

New Moon: starting new projects, dreaming new dreams, setting new intentions; plant the seed

Waxing Moon: brainstorming and planning; take enthusiastic actions

Full Moon: intense and sensitive time; illuminating and releasing what no longer aligns or serves your soul; identifying changes that need to be made, and a great time to charge your crystals in the moonlight!

Waning Moon: reflection time; reviewing and consolidating projects in preparation for the new phase

Journal and track your emotions and energy during the moon phases, to help identify your unique and individual responses and rhythms.

Planetary

Throughout the year, there are planetary cycles that impact and influence us here on earth. One of them which you may have heard of is Mercury retrograde. Three or four times a year, for three and a half weeks at a time, Mercury (closest planet to the Sun), speeds past Earth in what appears to us as if it's moving backwards or 'reversing.'

Imagine you were riding a bike and another bike rider passed you—you could tell that the other rider was going faster than you. If the other bike slowed down and you passed it, the other bike would appear to move backwards as you looked back. Imagine that the other bike rider then speeds up, kicking dust and pebbles, passing you again with turbulent energy. That turbulent energy is what we feel here on Earth, as Mercury speeds up again. That planetary dance is what many feel during those infamous few weeks, several times every year.

It's believed that when Mercury is resting, our energy and activities return to normal. But what does the retrograde period feel like? You may have noticed countless social media updates blaming everything from dysfunctional devices to misunderstood communications on Mercury retrograde. However, the truth is that it can be an inspiring and creative time.

It is said that we should avoid serious commitments, signing contracts, major purchases and irreversible or important life decisions during this time, but I don't believe we need to avoid these altogether. Simply take an extra few breaths before actioning these during Mercury retrograde. Let's remember that the energy we put into everything we do has great influence. If we spend all of Mercury retrograde expecting life to go wonky, it will!

Empowering and educating ourselves on the nature of our Universe is part of being a Soulpreneur. You don't need to know everything, but research what resonates. We are part of this wild and wonderful Universe; honouring her rules, rhythms and cycles creates much more freedom and flow throughout our business and life.

ENERGIES

Masculine and feminine

While we are on the topic of embracing universal cyclical energies, let's clarify the difference and equal importance of our masculine and feminine in business.

I had an aha moment on the flight to a Soulpreneur Circle in Melbourne reading Barbara Stanny's financial goldmine book, *Sacred Success,* when I read these lines: *The masculine in business asks 'show me the money'; the feminine in business asks 'show me how to help.'*

Personally, I believe we need a balance of both. There are times when our business requires our masculine energy, our yang. Focused on the money, admin, details, making stuff happen, goals, achievements, launching, selling, promoting, marketing, focus, strength, linear and logical facts and actions, direction, clarity, analysis and power.

Other times we are in our feminine, connecting in with the great mother, the divine feminine, our yin. In this energy, we are writing, creating, connecting, nurturing, nourishing, resting, receiving and surrendering. We are embracing creativity, intuition, gentleness, patience, faith, vulnerability, beauty, flow, spirituality, healing, grace and peace. Both have positives, both have negatives. We seek balance.

To activate your divine masculine:

> *go for a run or do some strength training*
> *stand tall on your tippy toes and reach up to father sky, letting him lead you*
> *eat grounding foods like nuts, seeds, avocados and root vegetables*
> *diffuse frankincense, black pepper or cedarwood essential oils*

To active your divine feminine:

> *attend a yin or restorative yoga class*
> *take your shoes off and let your feet soak up some Mama Earth*
> *spend time with your favourite flowers and crystals, and eat luscious light foods and fruits*
> *anoint yourself in rose, geranium or lavender floral essential oils*

Chakras

If you don't already know about the healing power of cleansing and strengthening your chakras, I highly encourage you to explore it. If you haven't heard this word in the yoga studio, you may have heard it on social media. Chakras are pretty trendy right now—and for good reason!

For thousands of years, mostly in Eastern cultures, it's been believed that we have seven major chakras represented by energy wheels in our bodies. The Sanskrit word 'chakra' translates to 'wheel' in English. Chakras have been brought into Western cultures by yoga teachers and energy healers.

Eastern cultures and practices believe that illnesses arise in the body centres when chakras are blocked or unbalanced. The seven main chakras to start exploring are:

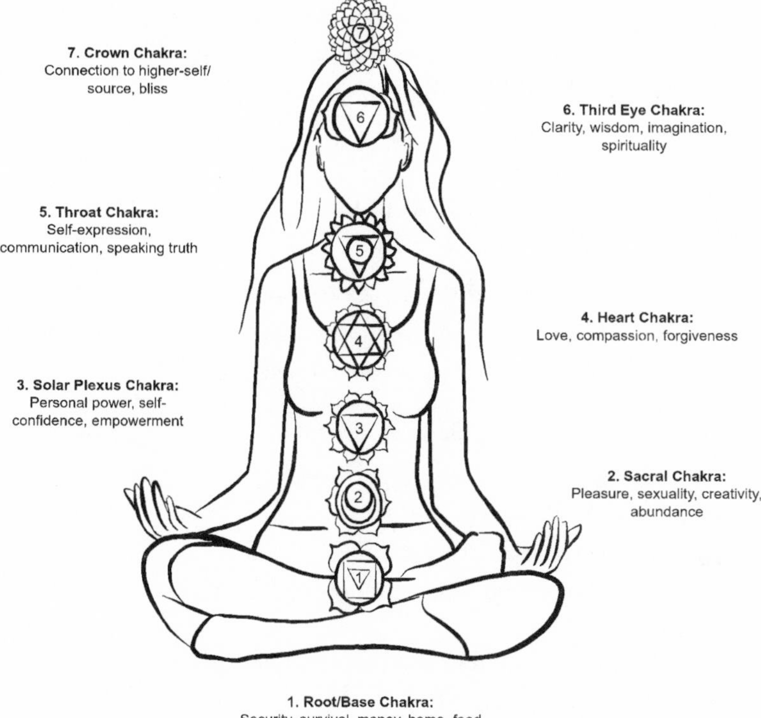

Getting to know (and clear) your chakras is a beautiful step towards emotional health, as they each represent an emotional centre.

During my cancer treatments, I loved learning about self-love and healing my heart chakra. I started by diving deep into my 'heart sores' (the past experiences and moments that were trapped in and slowing down my heart chakra). I unearthed and released the memories that were sitting heavily in my chest. This was followed by energy healing, reiki and chakra-clearing meditations, as well as wearing a beautiful heart-shaped rose quartz on a necklace over my heart chakra during my year of treatment.

It's wonderful to put this focused love and energy into the chakra that needs most care, but do look after all of them. We heal as a whole and healing is ongoing. It's also fun and deeply nourishing for our souls.

OTHER SPIRITUAL TOOLS

Crystals

Crystals aren't just pretty pieces to place in your office. They are powerful to use during healing sessions and in everyday life. Here are a few ideas for how you can use them:

> *Hold them or place them on specific chakras during meditations and visualisations.*
> *Sleep with them under your pillow.*
> *Wear them as jewellery.*
> *Hide little ones in your underwear or pockets.*

To get you started, check out this overview of common crystals and their healing properties:

> **Amethyst:** *powerful for energetic, emotional and spiritual healing*
> **Apache tears:** *confidence in facing health fears and making changes*
> **Aquamarine:** *calming emotions, confidently expressing and speaking your truth*
> **Aventurine:** *healing childhood wounds and nurturing your inner child to release the past*

- **Calcite:** *relaxation, meditation and strengthening your bones*
- **Citrine:** *attracting abundance and joy into your home*
- **Clear quartz:** *moves light and energy through our body, promoting clarity*
- **Fluorite:** *enhances mental health and decision-making*
- **Hematite:** *purifies and cleanses blood, powerful post-trauma or shock healer*
- **Jade:** *positive thinking, harmony and good fortune*
- **Moonstone:** *connects to our feminine, new beginnings and birthing our new life*
- **Rose quartz:** *self-love, acceptance, heart healing*
- **Selenite:** *cleansing energy, moving forward in a positive and proactive way*
- **Smoky quartz:** *powerful grounding to dissolve fears and anxiety*
- **Tiger-eye:** *enhances courage and clarity in decision-making*

Essential oils

Essential oils are aromatic compounds found in the seeds, bark, stems, roots, flowers and other parts of plants. They are the most pure and potent way to bring nature to us, and with us, wherever we go.

Since they have been a significant part of my healing journey, I've become so obsessed with essential oils that I have brought them into my business and teachings, especially after I noticed the positive influence on my clients. I even have an essential oils arm of my business.

Essential oils are nothing new to those of us who grew up in Australia with tea-tree oil for blemishes and mosquito bites, eucalyptus oil for a stuffy nose and whose grandmothers put lavender on pillows or in undie drawers. We now live in an exciting time as these little bottles of earth magic are being embraced and celebrated in a widespread way across the world.

I believe it's because we are craving a deeper connection with our Mother Earth more than ever before, so they are balancing out our earth disconnection and the increase in devices and the digital world. Yep, Mama Nature always aims to provide. She is always leaning in to heal, nurture and restore us, if we allow her.

Essential oils not only support us with their physical benefits, but they have emotional and spiritual properties too. Here are some suggestions for oils which can offer you soul support on your Soulpreneur journey:

> **Arborvitae:** *grace and faith*
> **Bergamot:** *self-acceptance and confidence*
> **Cedarwood:** *community and connection*
> **Clary sage:** *clarity and clear-sightedness*
> **Clove and Tea-tree:** *boundaries and cord cutting*
> **Frankincense:** *our ancient truth*
> **Geranium:** *love and trust*
> **Lavender:** *calm and communication*
> **Lemon:** *focus and alertness*
> **Melissa and Litsea:** *light and manifestation*
> **Neroli:** *uplift and connection*
> **Patchouli:** *grounding and peace*
> **Peppermint:** *lifting of spirit and refreshment*
> **Rose:** *love and heart healing*
> **Roman chamomile:** *peace and purpose*
> **Sandalwood:** *devotion and spiritual connection*
> **Spearmint:** *confident speech*
> **Vetiver:** *centring and grounding*
> **Wild orange:** *abundance and joy*

- **Wintergreen:** *surrender and letting go*
- **Ylang ylang:** *sensuality and playfulness*

You can also enjoy an essential oils masterclass here: www.yvetteluciano.com/bookclub

Oracle cards

We are lucky to have an abundance of oracle cards to choose from these days. From traditional tarot card decks that are based on a 78-79 ancient card system, through to the more open form of Angel and Affirmation cards.

I started playing around with tarot cards back in my teenage Goth days. It wasn't until many years later, when I was gifted Angel and Goddess oracle card decks to support me through cancer treatments, that I developed a deep respect for these powerful tools. I now have a collection of almost fifty oracle decks from around the world, including animal kin, angels, goddesses, Wicca, mythology, unicorns, ascended masters, faeries, dragons and all sorts of decks including several tarot decks.

My original decks are still my favourite so, rest assured, you only need one deck to get started. And they are easily and affordably available. What themes are you interested in? What calls to you?

How to select your oracle card deck:

- *Browse through card decks online or in bookstores.*
- *Select a deck which has an energy, colours, artwork and themes that call to you. This is a very personal decision, so trust your intuition to guide you to the deck you are destined to work with.*
- *Be aware that some decks have darker energies and messages than others. Personally, I do not use or recommend darker energy decks for those experiencing life-threatening illness or mental health challenges.*

There are plenty of light energy card decks that would be best during those times.

When your oracle deck arrives:

> *Open your deck, spread out all the cards and either smudge them with sage or lightly sprinkle with lemongrass, clove, oregano or tea-tree essential oil.*
> *Pull the card deck back together in your hands and shuffle, while setting an intention for the deck and the journey you are starting together.*

Spend time each day getting to know your deck and all the individual cards and meanings.

Your oracle cards will support you to explore your truth and receive guidance from your higher power. Have fun with them and enjoy the journey with your deck.

You can check out some of my decks and how to do your own reading here: www.yvetteluciano.com/bookclub

Journalling

Journalling (free-writing) is a powerful way to release past and present emotions, feelings and experiences. Allowing fully uncensored venting of your experiences, fears and feelings can work miracles. You never know where your journalling is leading and what incredible ideas might pour onto the pages.

There's only one rule: **let it all out!**

CONNECTING WITH THE SOUL OF YOUR BUSINESS

Through conversations with successful Soulpreneurs, I've uncovered different approaches to this very personal conversation.

Some, including myself, believe their work is an expression of their soul. However, I also believe that various different projects are almost separate to me, yet still a part of me, like children. A parent will always feel their soul is intertwined and inseparable from their children, even though they are two, not one.

Every event has its own soul. Every album has its own soul. Every book has its own soul. The soul of the Soulpreneurs work I do is different to Earth Events. The songs and albums I've written or released had their own souls.

Our job is to be the earthly custodian and guardian of our work. We are uniquely selected to bring it to life and to protect it, in the same way a parent raises and shelters a child.

Remember though, just because we are selected doesn't mean we have to respond to every tap on the shoulder. When we say 'no' or 'not now' to an idea, it may wait patiently. If it needs to make its way into the world urgently, it will find another opening, someone else for the job.

Don't take this as pressure, just know that what is meant to come through you will come through. If you don't do it, someone else will. Find peace in that. These divine assignments will find a way to be birthed somehow.

You will be relieved to know that you are only delivered assignments that you can handle.

SPIRITUAL BOARD OF DIRECTORS

Yes, you can handle what is sent, but you don't have to do it alone. Not only do we have support from our fellow Soulpreneurs here on Earth, but we have spiritual helpers: angels and spirit guides who are here to assist us and the soul of our work.

This is your **spiritual board of directors**, the archetypes who help you navigate career and business decisions. Call on them for the big questions when at a significant crossroads, or for small choices, from picking the colour of artwork to deciding the time of day to make an important phone call.

These powerful spirit guides help me connect with the soul of my business, keeping us close. Every morning before opening my laptop, I invite my spiritual board of directors to take the reins and join me for the working day. What shall we do, who shall we connect with and what shall we create?

At the head of the board is the spiritual CEO of my business, my guardian angel. By her side are people who I have loved here on earth but who have passed on, from great-grandmothers to people I never even met here on Earth, including Maya Angelou, Princess Diana and Wayne Dyer.

While I was in the middle of writing this book, a dear guitarist friend passed away. He had been a huge part of my music career. Through my tears and beach walks, listening to his amazing music and favourite bands on repeat, I invited him to be part of the book and to help me share guidance that would support other musicians. He has influenced so much of this book. (Thanks, Big D!)

By our sides and lighting our way are Archangels Michael, Gabriel, Raphael and Sandalphon. Not to mention Goddess Isis and Mother Mary, who have held me through so much. And the faeries that live in the trees between my home and the beach. Oh the faeries! What a journey we have been on together.

What a relief to know that we do not need to rely on our own strength alone. We walk this path alongside spirits and guides who are far more powerful than we can fathom in earthly form. These angels, guides and goddesses have been with us the whole time. They have guided you here, to this book, to this moment.

Something happened on the path of this book landing in your hands. Your guides ensured that you would receive this message in this moment. They want you to stop for a moment, close your eyes and take a deep breath, knowing that an unexplainable inkling you have (perhaps buried deep down inside) has called you deeper into your true path and purpose. Know that you are supported; these guides are holding you and guiding you. It's time to fully embrace them and welcome them into your career, business and life. Feel into who is with you as your spiritual board of directors.

> If you knew who walked beside you at all
> times, on the path that you have chosen,
> you could never experience fear or doubt again.
>
> – *A Course in Miracles*, Foundation for Inner Peace

On the next few pages are suggestions as to who you may feel beside you on this journey, with more tools available for you at: www.yvetteluciano.com/bookclub

Archangels

You do not need to be religious to work with angels or goddesses. I believe they are non-denominational and love to help everyone who asks and allows. They have been waiting your whole life to be invited in:

- **Ariel:** *animal kingdom and environment*
- **Chamuel:** *peaceful relationships with others and ourselves*
- **Uriel:** *wisdom and knowledge*
- **Metatron:** *spiritual wisdom and power*
- **Gabriel:** *communication*
- **Raphael:** *healing*

- **Michael:** *spiritual protection and life purpose*
- **Sandalphon:** *music*
- **Azrael:** *loss, endings and transitions*
- **Jophiel:** *beauty and self-care*
- **Haniel:** *joy and grace*
- **Raziel:** *bringing past lives, lessons and secrets into the light*
- **Raguel:** *justice and harmony*
- **Jeremiel:** *change and hope*

Goddesses

Goddess names, representations and meanings come from many different ancient cultures, mythology and pantheons (and are still practised in religions such as Hindu), including Greek, Roman, Egyptian, Celtic, Nordic and Sumer. Exploring the world of goddess culture can be truly amazing for Soulpreneurs who would like to learn more about and uncover the power of the Divine Feminine in their work.

Julie Parker, wise and wonderful founder of *The Priestess Podcast*, recommends exploring the following goddesses for business and personal development:

- **Abundantia:** *financial abundance and prosperity*
- **Aphrodite:** *self-love, self-esteem and self-confidence*
- **Artemis:** *sovereignty, self-confidence and leadership*
- **Athena:** *inner wisdom and strength*
- **Bast:** *independence*
- **Dana:** *manifestation and divine magic*
- **Freya:** *strength, belief and independence*
- **Gaia/Mother Earth:** *connection to nature, energy, working with cycles and the seasons*
- **Isis:** *leadership and self-empowerment*

- **Kali:** *transformation, courage and releasing fear*
- **Kuan Yin:** *self-compassion and compassion for others*
- **Lakshmi:** *financial abundance and prosperity, creating beauty*
- **Maat:** *justice, fairness, mediation and legal matters*
- **Mary Magdalene:** *love, compassion, leadership*
- **Ostara:** *rebirth, renewal and energy*
- **Pele:** *passion, commitment and strength*
- **Sarasvati:** *creativity and inspiration*
- **Sekhmet:** *strength and power*

Sige: the power of solitude, quiet and rest

Animal Kin

One of my dear collaborators, Sarah Wilder, works closely with our animal kin through her oracle card deck, a favourite in our Soulpreneurs circles.

Are there animals that you feel connected to or animals who have been popping up in your life recently? Perhaps there is an animal that you have an unexplainable fear of or recoil from? This could represent your shadow aspects.

Here is a start for you to start identifying your animal guides:

- **Bear:** *protection*
- **Bee:** *power*
- **Buffalo:** *gratitude*
- **Butterfly:** *change*
- **Camel:** *celebration*
- **Cardinal:** *passion*
- **Cat:** *independence and mystery*
- **Cow:** *nourishment*
- **Crab:** *trust*
- **Crow:** *magick*

- **Deer:** *grace*
- **Dog:** *forgiveness*
- **Dolphin:** *play*
- **Dove:** *peace*
- **Dragonfly:** *imagination*
- **Elephant:** *community and compassion*
- **Fox:** *solitude*
- **Frog:** *healing*
- **Giraffe:** *perception*
- **Goat:** *grounding*
- **Ibis:** *acceptance*
- **Jellyfish:** *flow*
- **Lion:** *courage*
- **Owl:** *intuition*
- **Peacock:** *pride and inspiration*
- **Pig:** *abundance*
- **Shark:** *instinct*
- **Snake:** *transformation*
- **Spider:** *dream weaver*
- **Starfish:** *sensitivity*
- **Swan:** *harmony*
- **Turtle:** *longevity*
- **Whale:** *communication*
- **Wolf:** *connection*

Two of my mythical favourites are the unicorn for miracles and the phoenix for resilience.

I'm not a woman. I'm a force of nature.
– Courtney Love

Embracing a goddess like Isis can fill you with fierce feminine power, while Kuan Yin will fill you with compassion and softness. Working with Archangel Michael will strengthen your soul, while Raphael will help your healing.

Let them in. Allow them to ignite these powers within yourself. Within your own soul.

Working with your angels, goddesses and deities will help power up your clarity, confidence and creativity. Do remember they are honouring and mirroring your inner power. In other words, it is all within you. You are the wise one. You are the sage.

Do not hand over power to other beings anywhere, whether in heaven, in spirit or on Earth. **That includes spiritual teachers!** You have free will and the power to make all your own decisions.

SURRENDERING TO SIGNS AND SYNCHRONICITIES

Our spiritual board of directors will deliver us everything we need through signs and synchronicities—sometimes small, sometimes grand, yet always significant. You will know when something is significant, because you will feel it.

Following the crumbs, trusting what is being shown to us, isn't about finding ourselves. This is about revealing ourselves, rediscovering the higher plan and vision of our life, the one we signed up for when we chose this body, this birth date, these parents.

You are not finding yourself. You are remembering the powerful source of light that you are, and the magic that has been within you all along.

At times we look for the obvious signposts, but little signs are like stepping stones. Little signs like following an unexplained feeling that may not make sense, going to an event or workshop, buying a book, visiting an art gallery or even watching a film, seeing a friend you haven't in a while, reading through old journals.

Notice what is calling to you. There may be signs in there waiting. Then notice the synchronicities. Did a friend you were just thinking about last night call you this morning? Did you wake up thinking about a particular book, then a review of it was the first post you saw on Facebook that day?

The more you pay attention to the signs and honour them, the louder, brighter and more noticeable they will become. Journal them. Share them with a Soulpreneur Buddy. This one can be fun! Help each other decipher and decode these guideposts along the map of your divine destiny.

Paying attention teaches us to be present and take notice. Never ignore the soul of your business, your angels, your guides and the Universe. They are all conspiring to deliver you the guidance you are seeking.

~ SOULPRENEUR SUCCESS SUMMARY ~

✓ *Learn and understand your natural cycles.*

✓ *Gather your spiritual business tools.*

✓ *Embrace the subtle energies you need to draw upon to run your business.*

✓ *Work consistently on clearing your chakras.*

✓ *Tune in to your spirit guides.*

✓ *Start journalling the signs and synchronicities.*

chapter SIX

The Greatest Career Investment

I've learned that self-care is more important than working yourself to the point of exhaustion. It keeps you creative and passionate.

– **Jessica Origliasso**

Self-care is the foundation of sustainable success for Soulpreneurs. As sensitive souls, we are not built to hustle and bustle our way through the nine to five (or seven to ten). Burning out is common for Soulpreneurs in their early years of business. I believe we are particularly susceptible, as we are so emotionally and energetically invested in our work and connection with our audience.

In this chapter, let's create a plan together and commit to serving the world in a way that also serves our physical, mental and spiritual health. You may be surprised how your creativity and career thrives, when you nurture yourself with self-care. This isn't just about a self-care Saturday or Sunday (which is a great start); this is about how we approach every single day.

STEPPING OFF THE HUSTLE BUS

With the fast-moving online entrepreneurial movement, we are seeing more glorification of hustling and pushing our way to our destination than ever before. Now if that feels good to you, go for it. However, if you want more peace and flow along the path to your purpose, you can choose another way.

This is a particularly important conversation for recovering overachievers (myself included), who have previously defined themselves by their success, achievements and accomplishments.

Ambition can be a wonderful thing. It energises our workday and powers up our productivity. However, I believe that the ambition driving our mind is not always in alignment with our body and soul. Which is how and when we hit burnout and breakdown. Our body is clever that way: she will slow us down and tell us when we need to go slow. Our mind loves the hustle, yet our body prefers to hum along.

Let's replace the social media quotes glorifying the hustle with something that feels better. New business buzz words. Take your pick:

Creativity	Flow	Gratitude
Ease	Focus	Presence
Energised	Grace	Productivity

These are the words that I prefer to anchor into my day and share. Choose what feels best for you. Peace, patience and persistence are a perfect formula for soulful success.

This doesn't mean that we need to stop working diligently towards our goals. There are times in our careers that require late nights and far too much laptop time. That's normal, yet should be occasional. Yes, you can still be highly driven, achieve big things and keep your sense of ambition intact.

Simply be mindful of the energy you choose, because you attract the audience, clients and abundance of that vibration. They will match your vibe.

A peaceful leader attracts a peaceful team. A healthy team is a thriving team.

Always remember that there is no work in this world that is more important than your own wellbeing. There are times when we all need this reality check! Remember that your health is your wealth.

KEEP BREATHING

Our human reactions to stress fall into three main categories: fight, flight and freeze. Which reaction feels most synonymous with your own response to stress?

None of these responses are 'wrong.' These are survival instincts that would have saved lives in our cavewoman days if, for example, an angry bear had entered our cave. Our bodies (as smart as they are) can't tell the difference between fear caused by a real and serious physical threat as perceived by our ancestors and a nasty email. Our natural reaction to feeling our life is in danger is the same, no matter where you are or what you are facing.

In all the above responses, a common feature is that we stop breathing properly. Whether to conserve energy or maintain stillness, the natural inhale and exhale of our breath is momentarily interrupted. This triggers a chain reaction of anxiety and adrenaline, so we must learn to remember to breathe.

Deep belly breathing during overwhelming or difficult moments is a wonderful gift and invaluable skill to learn. Best part? It's free and always available to you! Sometimes just remembering to focus back in on your breath can make all the difference—whether you are in your office, in a busy public space, on a hectic highway, or anywhere else where you feel stress.

All forms of **meditation** help us reduce the impact that stress and anxiety have on our joy and the quality of our lives. Meditation helps to improve our sleep, energy, fears, frustrations and even boosts our immune system. Mindfulness-based meditations include sitting meditations, transcendental meditation, prayer meditations, mindful movement and even walking meditation.

SOULPRENEUR STEPS

Try this deep breathing exercise and notice the **sense of calm** you can achieve. Start practising on a regular basis, to gain the benefits I mentioned above.

1. Sit up straight in a comfortable place, either on the floor in a cross-legged position or in a seat with both feet flat on the floor.
2. Place one hand on your chest and one on your belly.
3. Close your eyes.
4. Start to take big inhalations and even bigger exhalations.
5. Feel the hands rise and fall as you blow your belly in and out like a balloon.
6. Choose two words to breathe in and out on. My favourites are *peace*, *calm* and *safe*.

You can do this anywhere and you don't even need to close your eyes. You can look out a window or up at the sky. Use your hand to make sure you are still breathing deeply.

This exercise will ease you instantly. Essential oils like frankincense, lavender or vetiver will help calm and ground you.

Respiratory blends with peppermint and eucalyptus will support your airways.

If you prefer to be guided in this practice, I've created a free soothing meditation download for you here: www.yvetteluciano.com/bookclub

DIGITAL DETOX

While I'm grateful for the digital connection and devices that help me connect with so many souls, helping me build abundant businesses, we all need a little device downtime. Set yourself periodical breaks and digital detoxes: a weekend offline with no social media, no email.

NUTRITION

You're no stranger to the awesome reasons to nourish your body with wholefoods—whole, real foods that Mother Earth provides—foods that are scientifically and vibrationally high in energy, full of colour and life force. Unlike packaged or genetically-modified products that fill our supermarket shelves, wholefoods are unprocessed and unrefined, with minimal additives or other artificial substances.

Sounds simple, right? Well, it once was. For some time, it was harder to source the simple wholefoods our grandparents did. Nowadays, thanks to the healthy eating movement hitting the mainstream, we can source nourishing foods more easily than our parents' generation could.

Yes, it comes at a price. But what is the real price of purchasing cheap toxic products—processed, genetically-modified or sprayed foods? More importantly, if you choose to consciously consume animal products, how do we put a price on the animal's wellbeing during its life?

This book isn't here to dive down that rabbit hole. I believe in bio-individuality. There is no one diet that works for everyone, or for an entire lifetime. That is an ethical conversation to have with yourself, a naturopath, nutritionist or holistic medical practitioner. What I will discuss here though, is how nutrition impacts on our overall wellbeing, energy, intuition and your work as a Soulpreneur.

Let's check back in on the basics. Why should we eat well?

> *Boost your energy and lift your mood.*
> *Support you through scary and stressful times in your career and business.*
> *Improve your digestion and detoxification; let the past go.*
> *Deepen sleep to keep you rested, refreshed and sharp through your workday.*
> *Clear skin and desired weight.*
> *Boost your immune system to keep you strong and efficient.*
> *Nourish new healthy cells and new innovative ideas.*
> *Inspire others around you to adopt healthier foods.*

Tips to get started:

> *Set the vibe. Create a kitchen you want to spend time in. Essential oils, candles, positive eating affirmations and vibrant recipes on your fridge.*
> *Get to know your local farmers' market, health store or produce manager, or order online.*
> *Attend cooking classes—in person or online.*
> *Find healthy wholefoods chefs that you like. Follow them on social media and fill your kitchen with their books.*
> *Get your family, friends and Soulpreneur buddies involved. Cook for each other and share ideas.*

- *Have easy go-to meals for when you have an action-packed week.*
- *Eat before you go out, and always have a healthy snack in your bag.*
- *Stick to the outer parts of the supermarket where the produce and fresh food is, rather than the aisles containing packets and cans.*
- *Just because something is meat/dairy/gluten-free doesn't mean it's healthy. Fake meats tend to be highly processed and dairy/gluten-free foods can be packed with salts and sugars.*
- *Be aware of the high sugar content hidden in sauces, cereals and 'health' bars. It's not just about avoiding sweets and lollies.*

Have fun with different wholefoods, recipes, juices and smoothies. The keyword here is fun. Unless you have medical concerns, there is no reason to become super strict with your diet overnight. Sometimes a laugh with friends or my husband over a glass of wine at our favourite restaurant is exactly the soul medicine I need. You don't need to be 100% perfect. It ain't much fun and isn't sustainable in the long run.

Try to apply the 80/20 rule: 80% nourishing wholefoods and the other 20% favourite indulgences. The more fun you have with wholefoods, the more enjoyable they will become, nourishing and fulfilling you.

EXERCISE

We all know that exercise is important. Moving your body is part of being human and the nature of life. Even Richard Branson and Mark Zuckerberg have praised their workouts as being key to their success and productivity. Let's face it, any increase in exercise is awesome for our physical and mental health.

It's important to choose the right exercise for you, taking into account your current situation, stamina and advice from your health professionals. Haven't exercised for a while? Restorative or yin yoga, walking and swimming are great for most levels of fitness and stages of life.

For me personally, long walks on the beach are my favourite. Walking is not only totally free, but you can do it almost anywhere, at your own pace and for any distance. I love it that, regardless of how I'm feeling, walking is doable. Most days it's an 'hour of power' with pumping music in my headphones. Other days it is simply a short slow walk, then sitting in the sand listening to the waves.

TRYING NEW THINGS

Are you one of the lucky athletic types who love exercise? Maybe now is a great opportunity to explore slower-paced restorative styles? Perhaps you are someone who has never really been an 'exercise type' (I'm with you on this one!). I was never a fitness girl, which I now believe is partly responsible for a whole lot of past physical and mental health challenges. Since I adopted daily walking and regular exercise, I feel like a different person.

I never thought I would say it but, when I skip exercise now, I actually miss it. My anxiety rises, my energy drops, my mood is flat and I crave moving my body. I also start turning to junk foods. In short, I feel down in the dumps. So often, it's as simple as stopping what I'm doing and taking that walk wherever I am, bouncing on the trampoline to my favourite song, even dropping into some yin yoga stretches on my office or hotel room floor. Find what works for you.

As a side bonus, exercise also helped me weed out old social activities. Whenever I used to catch up with friends, it was 'let's go for a drink,' whereas now it's 'let's go for a walk' or 'let's try that new yoga class.' This transition may take some time. Like with everything, be gentle with yourself.

Every little bit of exercise and activity helps. One step at a time.

SLEEP

Insomnia and sleepless nights are common for Soulpreneurs. Most of us experience sleep difficulties at some stage, but this doesn't mean you're condemned to a life of fatigue and frustration. Try these top tips for a better sleep tonight:

Wind down

Are you guilty of taking a final scroll through Instagram right before bedtime? The artificial light from your phone—as well as laptop or TV screen—can mess with your circadian rhythm, so it's important to give yourself at least an hour of screen-free time before bed. Instead, read a book, try a basic meditation or tune in to your breathing.

Prep your space

How relaxed and peaceful is your bedroom? Ideally, it should be a dark, cool space with no distractions such as flashing lights or noise. Your body needs to cool down in order to fall (and stay) asleep, so room temperature is also an important factor. Ensure your mattress and pillows are free of allergens, and assemble your oil diffuser and calming crystals close to your bed.

Set a routine

You might think a daily sleeping timetable is just for babies—but think again. A regular routine will help set your body clock, meaning you'll get into a regular rhythm and intuitively know when it's time to rise and rest. Avoid heavy meals and caffeine close to bedtime and try to get to bed at roughly the same time each night.

Journal your thoughts

While lying in bed, if you catch your mind drifting to tomorrow's to-do list or recalling every regretful thing you've ever done, try scheduling in daily dump and reflection time, to get all of those thoughts out of your head. Just jot them down in a journal that no-one else will see and diffuse some oregano or burn some sage. Let it all go.

VITAMIN N

Disconnecting our devices and stepping into nature cleanses and restores our energy. The ultimate antidote to burnout is streams of sunshine on our skin, fresh air in our lungs and oxygen in our cells.

Nature calms, clears and replaces the clutter and confusion in our minds with soothing clarity, relieving stress and anxiety, reminding us what is truly important and restoring our vision and faith in the bigger picture. Our imagination can run wild and free, as Mama Earth has a magical way of filling us with new ideas, inspiration and breakthroughs.

Have you noticed that most of your best ideas have come while taking a walk, even looking out the window at trees or the sky on your bus ride home? Human beings' brains thrive in nature. She will reward you with better ideas, increased productivity and success in the long run. And the best thing about Mama Earth? She is entirely free and always present.

Keep an eye and ear out for the nature spirits and elementals who love to drop wisdom into your ears. Folklore tells us there are fairies, mermaids and devas hiding in the trees and waves, working with us within the subtle realms and co-creating a brighter, lighter planet. Ask them for guidance. Be open to receiving their whispers. The fairies will guide you in the garden, the mermaids will support you in the ocean. Graciously accept and act on the guidance that 'comes out of nowhere' when you are out there.

Believe. There are many notions our humble human brains can't yet comprehend.

EMBRACE THE ELEMENTS

Since the time of the ancient Greeks, our healers and tribes of ancestors have honoured the four elements of Earth, Air, Fire and Water. Scientist and philosopher, Aristotle, later added the fifth non-physical element of Spirit (or Ether). These elements are the building blocks of all life: our planet and our bodies.

When our lives are deficient in any of these elements, we mistakenly attempt to fill the void with other means. Instead of heading out to nature, we head to shopping malls or online stores for a quick fix—to fill a bottomless pit that never feels fulfilled.

It's like feeding hungry bellies with empty calories. While we may feel better temporarily, the hunger and cravings creep back, as we crave something with more sustenance.

Let's feed our bodies and souls with what we truly need. Let's embrace the elements and environment we were born into. Direct from Mother Nature: the creator of all elementals. The creator of us!

Balancing these elements can help you:

- *Restore your clarity and confidence*
- *Purify and release negative energy*
- *Boost your self-belief and creativity*
- *Connect back into your truth and inner wisdom*
- *Ease anxiety and lift your mood*
- *Enhance your office, home, altar and rituals*
- *Harness your intuition and natural superpowers*

THE PURPOSE OF EACH ELEMENT AND HOW TO INVOKE THEM

Earth

Grounded, supported and rooted; connected with Mother Gaia, the faeries, deer and wombat.

> *Walk barefoot in nature or hug a tree.*
> *Lay down in nature on grass or sand.*
> *Get your hands dirty by gardening or building sandcastles.*
> *Play with crystals. Hold them. Feel their textures, tune in to their energies and messages.*

Air

Winds of change and breath of fresh air; connected to the archangels, butterfly and eagle.

> *Deep breathing in nature where air is purest; near the ocean, on a mountaintop or in the countryside.*
> *Diffusing essential oils that clear the air.*
> *Open all doors and windows of your office and home to improve airflow.*
> *Drive your car with the windows down and enjoy the wind in your hair.*

Fire

Passion, fierce and fearless; connected with the goddess Pele, phoenix, cardinal and lion.

> *Light candles, selected by different colours and what they represent to you.*
> *Burn sage with a smudge stick.*
> *Where safe, ignite a fire in your fireplace or a bonfire on the beach (only if safe and approved by your local fire department).*
> *Soak up some sun (respecting sun safety).*

> *Write down all your challenges and anything you wish to let go, then burn it. Especially powerful at full moon but effective anytime.*
> *Get creative with arts or moving with dance.*

Water

Emotions, cleansing and flowing; connected with the goddess Aphrodite, triton, mermaids, whale and turtle.

> *Swim in a natural body of water (ocean, lake) or bathe with Epsom salts.*
> *Mindfully drink more pure, filtered water.*
> *Stand (or dance) in the rain.*
> *Mist yourself with a homemade spray containing filtered water and essential oils.*

Balancing these elements through your daily life doesn't need to be time-consuming or at all complicated. Stepping barefoot into your backyard, taking deep breaths and a big mindful glass of water, followed by lighting a candle at your desk and misting yourself with some essential oils will do just fine on a busy morning. The key here is respect and mindfulness.

Be grateful for these elements by welcoming them into your day and inviting:

> *The earth to ground and balance you.*
> *The air to breathe in new life and ideas.*
> *The fire to ignite your passion and fierceness.*
> *The water to keep you in flow and wash away what no longer serves you.*

Embracing the elements connects us to the core of who we truly are, which is much bigger than our temporary physical bodies.

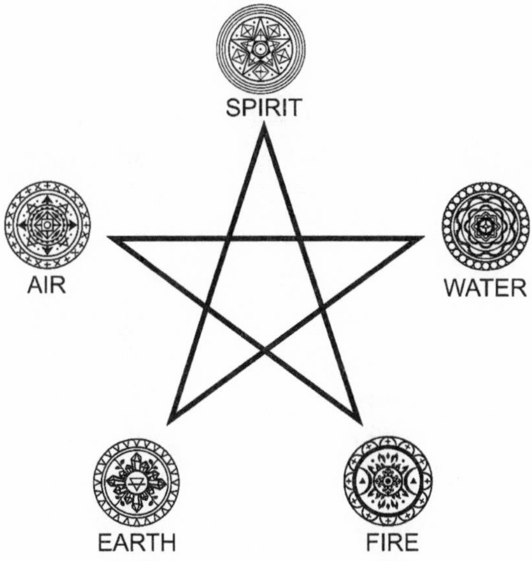

PROTECTING YOUR ENERGY AND PREVENTING BURNOUT

Soulpreneurs are notorious for burning out—physically, spiritually, mentally, emotionally. As such, adrenal fatigue is a common complaint in Soulpreneur circles, often caused by:

> *Overwhelm*
> *Saying 'yes' to everything and everyone*
> *Fear of disappointing people or missing out*
> *Trying to do everything and multi-tasking, instead of focusing on one thing*
> *Heavy workloads*
> *Juggling between babies, business and life*
> *Being an extra-sensitive empath, who needs more downtime and self-care*

How often do you say 'yes' when you know it should be a 'no'?

Fear of disappointing people

At the beginning of our careers, it's exciting to receive invitations to speak, perform and be interviewed for podcasts or media. What a blessing! I recommend saying 'yes' to anything and everything that is aligned at the beginning. But as your career develops, it's necessary to be discerning with your time.

After first checking in on whether the opportunity aligns with your values, audience and message, the next step is to explore the time and energy investment. Ask yourself: *Does this feel aligned with my priorities right now?* If it's an absolute 'yes' then go for it! If not, graciously decline. Always with generous thanks, well wishes, love and respect.

For people pleasers, this can be far harder than it sounds. So please ask yourself whether you'd rather live your life on other people's agendas or the path of your soul. This applies to all aspects of your life, not just your business. Once you master the art of a polite decline, you may be surprised how many new, far more aligned invitations come your way.

The Universe works in mysterious ways.

Fear of missing out (FOMO)

Whether it's a party invitation or a project idea, human beings have a deep fear of missing out—missing what may become the party of the year or the next trend in our industry. We RSVP 'yes' when we really don't want to go. We take on projects and 'opportunities' for the wrong reasons. And we find ourselves in careers and lives that are more in alignment with the agendas of others, than our soul's call.

All because we are afraid of missing out on something that was never destined for us in the first place.

We take these actions out of inner angst, anxiety and fear of making the wrong decision. Fear of feeling regret. Yet the only thing we end up regretting is doing the wrong thing for the wrong reason in the first place.

Social media has inflated the FOMO epidemic, as we are constantly exposed to what everyone is doing in their career, business or social life up to the minute. This layers on top of mainstream marketing campaigns that intentionally ignite and trigger FOMO as a strategic tool: the fear of missing out has been forced on us for our whole lives.

So what do we do? Remember that social media feeds are simply highlight reels, and that FOMO thrives from believing that others' lives are better than they really are. It's been suggested that FOMO is deeply rooted in our social status anxiety, one of our ego's powerful triggers. So work to find deeper peace and faith in believing that you are never meant to be anywhere but on your soul's path.

Join the revolution and embrace JOMO—the joy of missing out! Believe that not everything is meant for you, and there is a greater plan and vision for your life, whether that has to do with your work or your Friday nights. And trust in divine timing. Something might not be a 'no' for you, it might be a 'not now.' The Universe will bring it back into your life at a time that feels lighter, brighter and more aligned.

You know when something feels flat. Honour that feeling. Don't overthink it. Just let go of what doesn't serve you in this moment. Have faith in divine timing and what is truly meant for you.

Indecision

Are you feeling overwhelmed, working on multiple projects because you can't pick just one? I'm a recovering multi-tasker and it has transformed my business and life.

Reading Greg McKeown's book, *Essentialism: The Disciplined Pursuit of Less,* helped me understand how splitting my energy and focus on multiple projects was slowing them all down. He suggests it is best to work on fewer streams, but do them better, because every 'yes' has a cost.

You know that feeling when too many tabs are open in your brain? Let's close some of those down. Overwhelm crushes our free spirit and creativity. It takes away the space for new ideas and solutions to come through. Then there's overthinking, which crushes the beautiful simplicity and joy out of our projects (and lives).

For the overthinkers and multi-passionates alike, write **KISS!** (Keep It Simple Sweetheart) and keep it somewhere you'll see it every day. Do less and do it better. Stop complicating everything.

Stop starting things, start finishing things. Finish one meal before starting the next. Finish one book before starting the next. Complete one project before starting the next.

Now you understand that you're 'robbing' energy from one place to feed another, make sure you're clear on your priorities. Notice the trade-offs you're making.

While I still have a couple of different projects on the go, and probably always will because my creative spirit thrives that way, that's much less than I used to have going on! I also make sure they're at different stages. When I'm 'birthing' a new project, I ensure that all the other projects in my hands at that time are 'maintenance' projects with a different energy—that they are at the easy stage.

When I'm asked how I 'fit it all in,' I simply say that I don't. I'm discerning with all that I do. I do only the important stuff and there are sacrifices along the way.

I'm the first to admit that my email replies aren't as timely as they once were. And I rarely accept speaking or event invitations these days, especially if travel is involved. While it may disappoint some people, I know that all the time and energy I am placing into my books, courses and content will be of far higher service in the long run.

Any time left over is spent on my wellbeing, with my family, dogs or friends. I will not sacrifice a one-hour phone call with a dear loved one, for an extra admin hour of tending to emails. This is why the first person I brought onto my team is the angel who looks after these important admin elements of my business.

These are lessons that I learnt the hard way in my career: making the wrong decisions, choosing email organisation over content creation, and work flights over family time.

Be discerning with your time and energy. Focus on the real work, not the 'busy and bitsy' work. Fluttering around on Facebook may be important for your community connection, but don't let it disguise or distract you from your real work: creating, writing, healing, speaking, singing and teaching. The work you were born to do.

WE BECOME THE COMPANY WE KEEP

Have you heard Jim Rohn's famous saying: *You are the average of the five people you spend most time with*?

It's time to be mindful of who you spend your time with. Take a look around.

- *Are they lifting you higher and lighting you up?*
- *Do they fill you with comfort, hope and inspiration?*
- *Are they draining or depressing you?*
- *Do they take a toll on your time and energy?*
- *How do you feel after you spend time with them?*

Relationships

At the beginning of our journey into soul work, we may start feeling different and disconnected from everyone around us. For many Soulpreneurs this isn't a new feeling, having felt like an outsider for many years, regardless of the company we keep.

Personally, I have never felt like I fit in anywhere. Even back in my band days, Emmie and I used to laugh that we were too pop for the punk scene and too punk for the pop scene. Whether we were wearing combat boots to dance clubs surrounded by stilettos or pink tutus and glitter to Goth clubs, our band looked like a hybrid of Spice Girls and Marilyn Manson. It was the late 90s after all!

The same challenges arose when I started moving into the health and spirituality world—not being able to abide by the strict rules of the nutrition circles or what I originally perceived as the stereotype of being a spiritual person. Always feeling on fringe of every circle; always being that one step out of time, that smudge out of the lines, that little bit different ...

Although when I'm honest with myself, I now feel this is a story I'm attached to. Always being **determined** to be different. But that's a whole other story.

For you, for now, let's explore your feelings and support your experiences as you start your soul work. Especially if you are questioning who you are and where you fit in the world.

Inevitably, some of your **friendships will change** when you dive into your soul work. You're on the journey of a lifetime and you will crave friends who understand. Some of your friendships will grow stronger, others will fade away. And along the path, you will connect with a whole new circle of like-minded souls.

Value the quality of your friendships over quantity. Chances are you'll become more sensitive, more intuitive and your senses will be heightened when working with your soul. You'll crack open.

Soulpreneurs start to notice everything, including the energy and vibration of those around you. At times, you may obsess about bringing others on the journey with you. And some will come. Some of your friends may even be so inspired by your new work and commitment to your soul that they will grow with you every step of the way.

Unfortunately, that won't be everyone. And that's okay. Your friends don't need to be doing their soul work to stay your friends. You may notice that you don't spend as much time with some, or that you need to protect your energy a little when around them.

With those who aren't supportive of your new journey, choose not to speak about your new Soulpreneur path yet. If they are cynical, 'worried' or protective of you, think you have joined some cult or want to shelter you from potential 'failures,' simply don't talk with them about it. For the moment.

Deep down they might be worried about you changing so much that you'll leave them behind. (This can happen in romantic relationships too.) For the moment, just talk about them, talk about films or food, anything other than your soul work.

Take care that you don't let this happen to all your relationships, because it can be exhausting not sharing what you truly love and who you feel you are. Soulpreneurs can have a habit of leaking energy and depleting themselves. Be aware that many sensitive souls are generous and empathic, but your relationships deserve to be equally giving and receiving.

Beware of surrounding yourself with people who need your help, yet never take it; those who complain about challenges over and over, but never take responsibility or action in their own lives. Perhaps your innate healer wants to help them, and sometimes you'll be able to and feel valued in the friendship. Others (energy vampires, drama queens, chronic victims) will take advantage.

You need time and space to replenish your energy, and you cannot keep pouring all your love and energy into relationships that do not return the love. You cannot keep pouring from an empty cup. You need a mutual energetic exchange.

Healthy boundaries

Your heart chakra needs to be open to connect with your soul, your work and your people. But how can you protect yourself from leaking energy where you don't want to or receiving toxic energy that you don't want to call in?

It may be time to take a break from the people in your life who always talk about their problems but rarely ask about yours, or the people who drain you. The energy vampires.

Be mindful also with clients or audience members and don't blur the lines of the professional relationship. Avoid encouraging confusing or dependent relationships with your audience; it's not fair on either side. Create loving and friendly relationships, keeping them professional without spilling into the personal.

The empathetic nature of Soulpreneurs, whereby we are affected by the energy of others, leads to a life unconsciously influenced by others. It's likely you've always been a person who absorbs the energy of everyone in the room.

What are the signs that you're an empath? You most likely:

> *are highly sensitive and a great listener*
> *identify as an introvert who loves time alone (or a hybrid introvert/extrovert)*
> *are intuitive and experience 'gut feelings'*
> *are a generous giver, although not as comfortable receiving*
> *have strong senses and 'feel' the pain of all sentient beings*

Empaths are prone to feeling tired, being environmentally sensitive and highly emotional. They react strongly to the pain or drama of others' lives, either in person, on the news or even towards fictional characters in books and movies.

Empaths are attracted to working in the creative or healing arts, especially when it involves working with animals, art or nature. When working with people, they need to be aware of the energies they are accessing, because empaths can be unintentionally taken advantage of by very draining people.

As an empath, you may need replenishing in solitude, especially in nature. And as your career develops and thrives and more people want a piece of you, you will need to protect your energy.

Cutting energetic cords

Whether we chose to or not, we connect with other people through energetic cords. When activated, these cords exchange a stream of energy between two people until deactivated.

A healthy cord is one full of love, vibrancy and mutual positive energy exchange. An unhealthy or toxic cord is one of unequal exchange and is draining. The great news is that you can cut these cords and deactivate this energy drain with this simple ritual:

While visualising a sword energetically cutting the cords (perhaps that of Archangel Michael or Wonder Woman), smudge yourself with a sage stick (can be used like a sword), or enjoy a saltwater swim or bath, or place tea-tree or clove essential oil at the base of your neck. Frankincense is also an ideal essential oil to use regularly for this reason, as it has been used since the 16th century to ward off evil spirits.

Create your own ritual with the above tools, while saying: *Dear Guides, I am ready to cut energy cords that are not equally exchanging love and light. Please deactivate these cords now and surround me with healing light. Thank you.*

Daily rituals to shield your energy are recommended for empaths. Save your energy for your loved ones, your soul work and, most importantly, yourself.

Romantic relationships

The most prominent relationship of all, the one with your life partner, can face challenges as you awaken and align with your soul work.

Here are some suggestions for supporting your romantic relationship, as you move along the Soulpreneur path:

> *Dissolve expectations and remember your partner doesn't need to do everything with you—that's what your soul buddies are for!*
> *No-one is perfect. No relationship is perfect. Don't believe the hype you may see on social media around perfect relationships. The truth behind the scenes of some social media romantic relationships would make your skin crawl.*

- *Long-term relationships are rollercoasters. Roll with the ups, downs, highs and lows.*
- *Relationships require nurturing and sometimes healing. The grass isn't always greener on the other side; it is greener where you water it.*
- *Being passionate about your work, particularly in the early 'obsessive' days of a new business or project, means that you may not be as present with your partner for a while. Check in with them on how they're feeling about that.*
- *Enjoying healthy sexual experiences will open up your sacral chakra and not only deepen your relationship with your partner (or yourself) but also your emotions and creativity.*
- *Embrace forgiveness. Let go of past mistakes.*
- *Soul mates don't always agree on ego and earthly things. Your souls may be in alignment with the same values, but you still face earth obstacles and have different interests.*
- *As I once heard Louise Hay say: You don't like when people try to change you, so stop trying to change others. Resist the urge of wanting to 'fix' your partner, especially if you are a born healer. It is not your job to fix or heal your partner.*
- *All relationships serve a purpose, even the most painful and dysfunctional. However, if you feel your relationship may cross a line into abuse, addictions, manipulations, self-esteem or control issues, please seek professional support.*
- *Sadly, not all romantic relationships are forever. If yours ends, honour it. Honour your heart's healing. Grieve with grace, gratitude and lots of tears. And if you're seeking a new romantic relationship, be patient. Complete yourself first. There is nothing more attractive to a partner, than someone who is whole and fulfilled: someone who doesn't* **need** *a partner, but simply* **wants** *someone to share their beautiful life with.*

In the meantime, enjoy your Soulpreneur Buddy times and nurturing friendships. I don't believe in 'The One' soul mate. I believe we travel in soul families.

BALANCING BABIES AND BUSINESS

While your career and business may feel like 'your baby' sometimes, what happens when you also become responsible for real little humans? How do you find a balance between nurturing business and babies?

I am certainly no expert on this topic and, after speaking with many of our Soulpreneur mamas (and papas), I'm yet to find anyone who believes they are qualified to tackle this conversation. However common lessons and threads came up, when I asked members of our Soulpreneurs community and teachers:

> *Master the art of time management, adding in a heavy dose of presence and focus. I've seen parents get more done in a focused twenty minutes than the rest of us achieve in a full two hours!*
> *If possible, set up a separate dedicated workspace in your home, focused solely on your business. It can be a desk in your guest bedroom or garage. Anything to help you separate yourself energetically between work and family.*
> *Ask for help! Hire a cleaner or babysitter—or ask friends and family to help. Ensure they understand why it's so important you have this time to work on your business and build an even better life for your family.*
> *Let go of the guilt. We've experienced many 'mama guilt' tears at Soulpreneur retreats; emotions arise when children are left at home to enable focus on career and business. The consensus from fellow mamas is that your guilt doesn't serve you, your children or your business. It just gets in your way. Let it go.*

- *Set boundaries, implement self-care rituals, but be flexible with yourself. Squeezing in a mini meditation, as you sit next to your children while they drift off to sleep, can be just the soul fuel you need.*
- *Do what you can, when you can and where you can. Find the micro moments. Anything is better than nothing.*
- *Educate your children on what mama is doing, let them help, excite them about your passions and work in the world. Inspire them to believe in following their own hearts and dreams. You are their positive role model.*
- *Dissolve the expectations you have placed on yourself. Lovingly forgive yourself when things fall off the rails, whether it be the school lunches or your email inbox.*
- *Stop comparing yourself to other businesses and parents who appear to be perfect. We never know what is really going on behind the scenes. Almost no-one feels they have it altogether.*
- *Lastly, remember to prioritise what is really important to you.*

While we can aim to have it all, we must be at peace with not having it all at the same time. Your children will only be young for so long. Your career and business are not in a rush. There will always be opportunities now and in the future.

As Mother Teresa wisely said: *If you want to change the world, go home and love your family.*

~ SOULPRENEUR SUCCESS SUMMARY ~

✓ *Understand how you want to feel in your business and know that you can't serve others fully until you are treating yourself with ultimate care.*

✓ *Eat well.*

✓ *Enjoy regular exercise.*

✓ *Take tech-free time.*

✓ *Learn how to rest, relax, restore.*

✓ *Embrace nature.*

✓ *Practice regular energy cleanses.*

✓ *Nurture your relationships, especially your relationship with yourself.*

chapter SEVEN

Your Audience Awaits

You have to respect your audience.
Without them, you're essentially standing
alone, singing to yourself.
– K. D. Lang

WHO ARE YOU SERVING?

Your intended audience, your clients, those beautiful people waiting for you to rise up, they might not know you right now, but they're probably already searching for what is waiting to burst out of you.

While it's lovely to want to help everyone, focusing your love and energy on a specific group is a much more effective way to go. There's something special about having people who feel that you are completely devoted to them. You can be totally authentic, as you're not trying to be all things to all people.

It's a wonderful feeling to know that the audience you're attracting is an aligned fit for you, so let's explore 'niche' and all the abundance that comes with the practice of focusing in.

A niche doesn't always mean gender or age. It may be a common challenge or dream. Of course, you can consider important details like age, gender, where they live, whether they're married or have kids, but also their fears, challenges, beliefs, hopes and dreams. The deeper you dive, the more clarity you'll have on your direction, and the more detail about who you're here to serve.

When you get clear on your **who**, you can easily create useful products and services for those people simply by closing your eyes, visualising and empathising with your exact audience and knowing how they feel and what they need right now.

SOULPRENEUR STEPS

It's time for our next visualisation, where you'll **design and describe your audience**, and imagine their dream product or service.

Have your journal and pens handy for afterwards. And remember, you can record this script yourself and play it back, because you'll have your eyes closed throughout.

Seat yourself in a comfortable position and close your eyes. Take some deep belly breaths and start your visualisation with an open mind. Keep up those belly breaths.

Visualise your audience. Think about one specific person, the person you want to help most. Imagine just one member of your audience. Let them drift into your mind. Look at them. Are they male or female? What age are they? Start to visualise them clearly: their hair, their eyes, their clothes. What are they like?

Imagine where they are. Where do they live? Are they in a big buzzy city or a peaceful quiet town? Which town or city or country? Are they in a house or an apartment? Look for clues in their environment. Are they married? Do they have children? Do they have a job or business? Are they a full-time parent? What is their job? Whatever they're doing, do they like it? What is their experience in their occupation? What do they do with their time each day? How do they feel when they are doing what they do?

Move into other areas of their life. How do they sleep? What do they eat? How much movement do they do in their day? How is their health, both physical and mental?

How do they feel about their relationships, with their partner, their friends, their children, their parents, within their community? How do they feel about their life? Do they feel deeply connected? Are their relationships one of the best aspects of their life or an area where they really struggle and experience a lot of challenges? Imagine how they behave.

What's their financial situation? Is there abundance and freedom in finances, or scarcity, fear and tightness around money? Are they somewhere in the middle, where they're comfortable but not necessarily able to invest in everything they'd love to do?

Think about this audience member's fears. What keeps this person up at night? Is it money, family, health problems of their own or a loved one, issues at work, challenges with their business?

Now onto their desires. What do they secretly crave in their life? Is it better health, more fulfilling relationships or friendships, more energy, deeper peace, comfort or inspiration?

Consider their challenges. When they worry, are they anticipating something in the future or dwelling on something that happened in the past? What do they stress about? What are their greatest challenges? Is it something in particular or a general feeling of confusion and overwhelm that everything is getting too much? Are they big dreamers?

Visualise how they go about their day. What are their first thoughts in the morning? What is their greatest hope for the day ahead? Is it a new healer who finally helps them, a personal trainer who totally gets them, a clear direction on what to ask their doctor, an opportunity to connect with like-minded souls and have some fun, a business breakthrough that leads to abundance, a pay rise or promotion, funding for a major venture, a book that changes their whole perspective, a tool or a practice that helps them move through their fears, or simply that the kids eat everything in their lunch box?

Explore their greatest fear for the day. Where do their anxieties or challenges come from?

Watch their day in detail. From getting out of the shower, making coffee, getting ready, looking at themselves in the mirror, walking out the door or to their home office, driving the kids to day care or commuting to the office, how does their day unfold? What happens for them?

Which moments light them up? Is it smiles or kisses from their family, sunshine on their face, reading blog posts, seeing inspiration on their favourite Instagram account, receiving a phone call from a friend, or getting juice at their local cafe?

Take a look at the other side. What moments drain them? Is it screaming children, negativity online, the news, energy-sucking family or friends, an unappreciative boss, frustrations in their business, doctor's waiting rooms, being stuck in traffic, or the way they feel when they look in the mirror?

Reflect on the moments that light them up and drain them. Question how these relate to their greatest hopes and fears. Are their stresses one-off or ongoing? What do they complain about to their friends? What do they ask for advice on most?

Visualise this person sitting at a computer or on their phone searching for information. What are they typing into Google? What burning questions do they have? What are they seeking? Is it vibrant health, a deeper spirit practice, connection, an abundant career, friends who get them, a happy healthy family, or a proud feeling when they look in the mirror? How do they want to feel when they have it? What product, service or offering would help them?

When the Google search comes up, imagine it clearly. See your audience member arriving on a webpage or blog post and seeing exactly what they need to see to make their dream come true. The solution to their problems, the answer to their prayers, the fix for their complaining.

What is their ultimate solution, the offering, the product, the service that will help them through their challenges and bring their dreams to life? Is it an instantly downloadable audio, video, ebook, digital course or program? On what topic? Is it a physical product like a skin or food product, a beautiful piece of artwork or soulful jewellery? Is it an experience like an event with a community of like-minded souls or a one-on-one session where they are healed or given direction?

This is your webpage. What is it that they find and instantly know it's their dream come true? They are amazed. It's like you were reading their mind. They know this is their opportunity. This is going to change everything. This will fix everything.

Think outside the box. What has never been created for them before? Get clear on the feeling. What one word describes how they feel when they see your offering on that webpage? What gives them butterflies and sends them rushing to find the sign-up or buy-now button? And they do! They are in! What part of their life will never be the same after this? Why is your audience member over the moon that this offering exists?

Imagine their experience of working with you. What do they tell their friends about you? How has your offering changed their life? Why do they start recommending you to others and posting about it all over social media? This beautiful person is becoming your most loyal customer. This audience member is going to go out and tell everyone about you.

When you are crystal clear on who they are, what they look like, what their life is like and their greatest challenges and dreams, then go on to focus on the offering that you can create to heal, help, comfort or inspire them.

When you are finished, open your eyes.

Now in your journal, **write down everything that came to you clearly** in this exercise straight away. Once you have done that, go back through the above questions and jot down notes as you go, filling in more details. If you like, put on some music that captures the energy of your audience and the offering.

You can return to this exercise again and again to help you revisit old offerings or clarify fresh ideas for your audience. The deeper you dive, the more clarity you will have on the products and services you know your perfect audience will love. Some additional questions to explore for your audience follow, with space to jot down your responses.

Describe your **audience demographics** including age, gender, where they live, marital status, income, interests, hobbies, occupation, kids:

....

....

....

....

Describe the **personality** *of your audience, including values, favourite books, shows, websites and what they are looking up online:*

....

....

....

....

How does your audience **want to feel**? *What are their fears, challenges, beliefs, hopes, dreams and world views?*

....

....

....

....

What **stresses them out** *and keeps them up at night?*

....

....

....

....

What do they **secretly wish for**? *What are their wildest dreams?*

....

....

....

....

What **common life experiences** *or background do you and your audience share?*

....

....

....

....

Who do they **love** *and what do they* **buy** *already?*

....

....

....

....

How are you **similar and different** *to who they already love and what they already buy?*

....

....

....

....

Do they prefer **aspirational high end** *or easily accessible* **affordable products** *and services?*

....

....

....

....

Are you covering their **dreams***, their* **challenges***, their* **hopes***, their* **frustrations***? Are you crystal clear on who they are, what they want, and why you want to help them?*

....

....

....

....

Now start focusing in on **what you can offer them**. *Walk through what your audience needs and what you can give them. Write everything below. For example:* ***coaching, consulting, classes, digital products, physical products, events.***

....

....

....

....

Do these products exist in the market? Which products are your audience **already buying** *and from whom?*

....

....

....

....

*What makes you or your products different? What do you bring into the mix—is it a personal experience? What is your twist—your WOW—***your uniqueness***?*

....

....

....

....

What does your audience need that **isn't yet available** *or accessible to them?*

....

....

....

....

Which products or services could you **start creating right now***?*

....

....

....

....

Which products **feel easiest** *for you to work on? Which products align with your talents and Truth Trifecta?*

....

....

....

....

Remembering that there needs to be an ease and joy in creating these, what **feels good for you** *and utilises your natural gifts and talents? (The simpler the better!)*

....

....

....

....

Which products or services would **help your audience most***? Which will help solve their problems, ease their pain, fill them with hope or joy and inspire them to be happier or healthier?*

....

....

....

....

With those questions answered, it's time to **start researching.** Ask some of your existing or intended audience about these new products and services you would love to offer them. When you hear their views, reflect on whether your intuition was right. Is this product idea what they need? Is it at the right price point? Do you need to tweak? Research, research, research and record your findings here or in your journal:

....

....

....

....

....

....

EMPATHY AND UNDERSTANDING

Now let's unlock the number one secret to soulful marketing, which you can start doing today for free. This is the key to how I've worked successfully with those who have crossed my path over the last fifteen years, from bestselling authors to world famous rock stars. I believe this is better than any other strategy out there.

As a Soulpreneur, it will come super easily to you because you're a sensitive soul, someone who feels deep love and compassion with your audience.

The simple secret is one word: **empathy**. Empathy is your ability to understand and share feelings with other people. And in this case, the other people are your audience.

There is no business coach or marketing guru out there who can teach you anything more valuable than what you already have inside you. Your natural ability to understand the lives, highs and lows, hopes, dreams and challenges of your audience is everything. And your ability to understand their feelings will help you go far.

Although it's vital to think about the **why** in your career or business (as we did earlier in Part One), don't underestimate the importance of having clarity about the **who**. This not only helps with your marketing but, when you're super clear on who you're serving, it keeps you motivated every single day. It will also keep you moving through your fears, because you'll feel so deeply devoted to the people you want to help in the world.

Make sure you go deep into how your audience feels in your notes from the exercise you've just done. Understand how they feel, what their values are, what challenges they face, what they need, and what you can do or show to help them feel the way they want to feel.

Use your sensitivity, personal experiences and intuition to feel this connection. Combined with top level marketing strategies, you'll be absolutely unstoppable in making the world a healthier, happier place.

COMMUNITY AND BELONGING

> Never doubt that a small group of thoughtful,
> committed citizens can change the world;
> indeed, it's the only thing that ever has.
>
> – **Margaret Mead**

Whether you are building a blogging audience or a music fan base, the same community principles apply. This is about belonging. Like most animal species, we crave belonging. We want to feel part of a pack. Humans are naturally social creatures.

In his studies, social researcher Hugh Mackay identified that it's in our human nature to be social creatures who congregate as part of our cultural DNA; that we are not good at surviving in isolation; and that we are best in communities as they support and sustain us.

Personally, through working with unique beings (the 'misfits' and the 'outcasts'), I have seen that many of us have experienced a deep unhappiness and loneliness in the world, an emptiness from feeling that we don't fit in anywhere. Alienation, isolation, separation. Many grow up that way. Others experience these feelings later in life, as they seek a different life path and disconnect from the mainstream.

In short, humans crave connection and community. Your clients, customers, readers, viewers, fans and followers want to feel a sense of belonging to your community. They want to feel inclusion, sisterhood, brotherhood, comradeship, unity. They want to feel that they are finally home: that they have found their people, their shared values, their soul family.

We love to feel like we belong to something far bigger than us. Religion and churches have recognised this for centuries. As have organisations from sports teams to rock bands to comic book conventions! For your specific community, this may be in your online groups, in-person events or gigs where they can breathe a sigh of relief and a burst of excitement to finally fit in. Not just with you, but with the rest of your community.

When I was underage and sneaking into music gigs, I felt like I'd finally found home. These were my people; this was my place in the world. While I now appreciate almost all music, at that time it was the more punk, the dirtier, the grungier the band, the better. I didn't want mainstream, I didn't want the same music or bands that everyone else was listening to. I wanted darker, louder.

This is why niche is so important and why not trying to be everything to everyone will help you create a loyal audience. Focus on going deep, not wide. You could have 10,000 casual followers, who never engage with or buy from you, giving you the occasional 'like,' or you could have 1,000 dedicated community members, who engage and buy everything you do. They share your work with their friends. They are proud to be part of your community and sing your praises from the rooftops! Which would you prefer?

Building an audience of 'super fans' has always been a core part of music marketing. Back in my teenage days, I loved being part of street teams where the band you loved gave you free tickets, albums or 'merch' in exchange for promoting their gigs in your local area by delivering posters or flyers. As this was well before the social media boom!

The best part wasn't the free stuff. It was bigger than that. Something that money couldn't buy: feeling part of the band's team. A band T-shirt was so significant—the ultimate badge of the band and brand. It told the world: *This is who I am, this is who I identify as, and these are my values, my passion, my soul. This is my community, my family, my home.* We see this throughout the health, spiritual and wellbeing worlds too, with members wearing certain jewellery or activewear.

We will dive deeper into this in the chapter on branding later, although a community is much more than just a branding element.

Soulpreneur members frequently tell me how grateful they are for our community, which they didn't even realise would be one of the most powerful outcomes. It's not about the teachers or the training, but connection, the friendships, the community, the camaraderie. This is a great reminder for all of us: as the leader of the community, it isn't really about us at all.

A true leader doesn't need to be always **on**, or always sitting on their pedestal. I believe in leading from the middle and leading by example. As leaders, we take the risks first, learn the lessons first, dive in first. We create the space, we facilitate the groups, and we do the earthly things, the emails, the calls.

Once we create a space that organically and authentically attracts the souls that are aligned with the vision, the mission, the values, then the souls will come. Be the leader, of course, but then let the community connect. Just like you wouldn't interrupt every conversation at your party, try to not jump into every thread in your community's forum. Let your people share and find themselves and carve out their friendships.

Be an empowering example. Inspire with integrity. Communicate clearly who you are and what you value. And let your community align.

LISTEN TO YOUR COMMUNITY

After you start attracting your people, listen to them. Ask them questions, get to know them better. What do they want? What do they love about what you're creating? What could help them better? Serve them more? Ask them these questions directly. Surveying your community takes the guesswork out of the equation and is a useful tool when done in a personal way that aligns with their vibe.

~ SOULPRENEUR SUCCESS SUMMARY ~

✓ *Visualise your aligned audience member.*

✓ *Get down to details on who they are and what they want.*

✓ *Use your empathy to explore your audience's true desires.*

✓ *Carry out concrete research.*

✓ *Consider how you will bring these like-minded individuals together as a community that connects and supports one another.*

✓ *Survey your community.*

part TWO

Courage

chapter EIGHT

Step into Your True Power and Potential

I'm not afraid, I was born to do this.

Joan of Arc

The greatest strength and not-so-secret weapon of all successful Soulpreneurs is courage and confidence. Believing in yourself is the golden rule of Soulpreneurship, and also one of the greatest challenges for sensitive souls putting themselves out there in the world.

I don't believe that a lack of business know-how is what holds Soulpreneurs back. I believe it's lack of confidence, courage and self-belief. So let's work together to rewire what you believe is possible for you.

YOU ARE LIMITLESS!

When I first started following the call to create Soulpreneurs, I was in a meeting with James Colquhoun, founder and filmmaker of Food Matters and FMTV. I was sharing my Soulpreneurs course vision with James, and inviting him to come on board as one of the guest teachers.

The greatest gift James gave me that day was when he looked me straight in the eye and reminded me: *Your only limitation is the one you place on yourself.* He invited me to explore where I was playing small, and what limits I was self-imposing on the Soulpreneurs program.

The fact is that we are limitless. At least, we choose our own limits. So what determines the height of the glass ceilings we create for ourselves?

In his Soulpreneur classes, James referred to Dr. Bruce Lipton's studies on how we, as humans, inherit our belief system of what is possible through generations of genetics. These beliefs are stored deep in our subconscious mind, yet come to play in every part of our career and life. We not only inherit and download the DNA of our parents' and grandparents' physical conditions, but also their fears and behavioural conditions.

Does this mean that we not only inherit our height and eye colour from our parents, but also what we believe is possible in our lives? And this inherited expectation deepens when we spend time with people who have the same limiting beliefs, enabling us to get stuck in a never-ending cycle, which we then pass on to our children?

The good news is that, just like our physical health, these mental and emotional settings can be reset, thanks to the power of epigenetics. If lifestyle and environmental factors can influence our biological gene expression, what is possible for our inherited mental patterns, beliefs and behaviours?

Epigenetics is the study of changes in organisms caused by modification of gene expression, rather than alteration of the genetic code itself.

Dr Bruce Lipton is a leader in the epigenetics field. He believes that every person on the planet has the opportunity to become whoever they wish to become, complete with unimaginable power and the ability to operate from, and go for, the highest possibilities. He believes that we all have the power to break free from our inherited programming.

The first step is to recognise that our subconscious mind exists and has been influencing us. Hypnosis and kinesiology has helped me greatly with this.

You may also wish to use Siberian Fir or Douglas Fir essential oils, as part of your generational healing rituals. These oils will help you reset your internal hard drive, where the belief systems of your ancestors are stored, allowing you to create your own belief systems and dismantle those glass ceilings.

GET TO KNOW YOUR EGO

> The ego is a fascinating monster.
>
> – Alanis Morisette

Your ego, your small self, your shadow self, your dark side, the devil on your shoulder, the gremlin in your head, your inner critic ... take your pick what you call him (or her!), but we all have one.

You may know this instinct by another name. Yes, the ego is also known as your shadow self, the negative naggers in your head, the devil on your shoulder, your inner critic. Whatever name you call it, it's likely to have held you back in the past. And the only way you can deal with it is to make peace with your shadow and bring it into the light, which can be emotionally challenging.

Your ego does not like you following your heart, starting your dream business or going to the next level. You will be cracked open and old insecurities and sensitivity will be triggered into past stories, limiting beliefs, blocks or self-esteem issues. An unconventional career path ignites our ego because our major fears as humans are humiliation and feeling unloved, which we are more vulnerable to when pursuing soul-led careers.

Stepping out as a Soulpreneur, you are vulnerable and open to criticism, which is especially hard for us sensitive souls. Expressing yourself, sharing your creativity, going for goals and visions that others might not yet see or believe in, and being seen and heard as your true authentic self is scary, but that fear is natural.

It's also a natural survival mechanism for your ego to try to protect you, by playing small and staying away from the spotlight. Looking at your insecurities may not be easy, although working through years of limiting beliefs will be totally worth it. After all, how will the world and your audience believe in you, if you don't believe in yourself?

To protect you, the ego tells you stories about being unworthy, about money, about being seen, being heard, being successful. It tries to tell you about how successful you are or are not 'allowed' to become. The ego clings on to old failures, flops, stories and success limits and, as a result, you can get stuck in patterns and behaviours that most Soulpreneurs will recognise: overwhelm, perfectionism, imposter syndrome and outdated limiting beliefs that have been with you for years.

It's common to overthink everything, and create problems and blocks that don't exist anywhere but in your head. Other common thoughts that the ego clings onto, to make you stay safe, are not being:

> *good enough*
> *smart enough*

> *pretty enough*
> *qualified enough*
> *connected enough*
> *young enough*

In short, never **enough** of anything!

As Ellen DeGeneres has said: *I work really hard at trying to see the big picture and not getting stuck in ego. I believe we're all put on this planet for a purpose, and we all have a different purpose ... When you connect with that love and that compassion, that's when everything unfolds.*

The secret to overcoming your ego or inner critic is knowing that **everyone** feels this way at times, even your heroes and role models, and that you can acknowledge these voices and fears without acting on them. The trick here is the simple knowledge that **it's okay to feel your fears.** You can coexist. Just don't let fear take the steering wheel or hijack your plans, because you have a higher purpose to fulfil here. Always remember that.

Of course, nobody does this perfectly all of the time. You may be shocked by the kinds of insecurities that even your heroes have, and what their inner critics tell them. Occasionally, you may be rerouted by your fears taking over.

We're about to learn now how to explore and acknowledge our fears, then course correct by reframing them, turning back towards faith. While we never become 100% immune to fears of humiliation or judgement, we can work to identify and diffuse fears as they arise. Transitioning from fear to faith is a daily choice we make as a Soulpreneur.

So, now you know what you're facing, let's look at how we can start diffusing those fears as they arise.

SOULPRENEUR STEPS

Bravely face those negative thoughts in your head that are holding you back from your true purpose and potential as the Soulpreneur you are destined to be. It gets easier with practice, so you'll return to this work over and over again.

Answer the following **reflection questions** in your journal.

> *What is a thought or belief that is holding you back? For example:*
  - *I regularly overthink and overanalyse.*
  - *I freak out about what 'everybody' will think of me.*
  - *The risk of failure holds me back from trying.*
  - *I procrastinate.*
  - *I'm a perfectionist.*
  - *I'm scared of vulnerability, rejection, people making fun of me, criticising me or not liking me.*
  - *I'm worried about getting lost in a crowded marketplace.*
  - *I fear that I will be embarrassed or ashamed by my ideas failing.*
  - *What if nobody pays attention or even notices me?*
  - *I feel like I'm behind everyone else in my industry.*
  - *I am uncomfortable with being visible and 'out there.'*
  - *I worry that I will never make as much income as I would in regular or current employment.*
  - *I'm not comfortable making money from something easy or something I enjoy. Work should be hard.*
  - *People in my life will be shocked or upset if I change. They will judge me.*
  - *I am scared to reveal who I truly am and what I truly want.*
  - *I'm not sure that I am smart/experienced/qualified/spiritual/pretty/young/old/healed/perfect enough to do this.*

> *How did this thought or belief arise?*
> *What exactly is this thought or belief blocking in your life?*
> *What is the old story that you keep telling yourself?*
> *Who do you compare yourself to?*
> *Who are you worried about 'being seen' or judged by?*
> *How does this thought or belief influence your actions?*
> *When have you let this hold you back or keep you 'small'?*
> *What does it 'cost' you?*

Now that you've explored what's holding you back, here is **a ritual for dissolving the fear** and busting through the procrastination. No need to record this one, as it's a quickie!

Close your eyes and take a deep breath. Visualise how it would feel if the thought or belief that you wrote down vanished. How would it feel to be free of this fear? What would you do today, if this thought dissolved?

You may be feeling a little anxious, tight-chested or heavy from this work. That's totally normal. Have a cry, go for a walk, then feel it, journal on it and let it move through you. The hard part is over and now we're moving on to how you can reframe these beliefs into helpful thoughts that will get you ready to dive into business.

COURAGEOUS AND CONFIDENT BELIEFS

All of this may seem a little unconventional and unexpected in a business book. However, you can know all the whiz-bang marketing, PR and digital strategies yet never reach your true potential, if you don't believe in yourself and dissolve this baggage that no longer serves you.

Let's take your old limiting and false thoughts and beliefs and reposition them into positive ones, simply with language. This is how courageous and confident beliefs can make you feel.

Create new positive beliefs and affirmations, such as:

> *The Universe has my back; my life flows effortlessly.*
> *It's always easy for me to make money.*
> *I deserve a career and life that I love.*
> *I am wildly successful in whatever career I choose.*
> *I am comfortable with creating and expressing myself.*
> *My dreams are in the process of coming to life.*
> *My new life has already begun.*

SOULPRENEUR STEPS

Explore how you can positively reframe your own limiting beliefs into helpful thoughts. For example:

I'm not really a writer, no-one will buy my work and it's a crowded marketplace

transforms into …

I am excited to courageously share my unique voice, experiences and message through my ebook. I am joining the other great teachers in my field in a growing and abundant marketplace.

Now it's your turn.

....

....

....

....

....

COMFORT ZONE

Soulpreneurs live most our lives outside of our comfort zone. Taking risks and feeling uncomfortable outside of what is familiar, safe, cosy and secure.

This can be challenging considering that humans are wired to seek comfort and safety, so balance this work with lots of self-care, to help support you through the stress and tension of living outside of your comfort zone.

It isn't easy, but it sure is exciting!

YOU'LL NEVER FEEL READY!

Starting **before** you are ready is the best and only real option. If you wait to feel entirely ready, you will never begin. Simply start and figure it out as you go.

I have never felt adequately prepared or ready for anything that I have launched or adventures I have undertaken. It's the secret behind all the most successful Soulpreneurs I know. In fact, many of us still don't feel ready for the work we are doing in the world today.

GET SUPPORT

This is where your fellow Soulpreneur family is so important. We all need support from like-minded souls who understand the highs and lows of sharing our soul's work.

Connect with other Soulpreneurs online or in person. And get professional support from kinesiologists, counsellors and coaches to help you move through blocks.

PURPOSE OVER POPULARITY

Stop sacrificing your soul for other people's approval or the need to be popular! You can never be everything to everyone. We can all get stuck in a trap that keeps us on the hamster wheel of life, going around and around in the same circles, saying the same things, buying into the same dreams, the same clothes, the same cars (clothes we don't want, cars we don't need) and careers we never desired in the first place.

Without healing this need for approval, to fit in, to be popular and to be liked, we will never fulfil our true soul call. Fears of being disliked or getting bad reviews are unhealed wounds that keep us small. They will stop you from starting your business in the first place, stop you from changing careers and stop you writing your book or releasing your album.

Previously I've had moments when I've stood at the back of a sold-out 1000-seater room at my own business' events, wondering how the message had become one that was so different from my own truth. These moments have occurred at some of my most successful, sold out, profitable and popular events, and they've felt gross, as they weren't aligned with my soul. They were fuel for my ego and food for my bank account. And while those reasons aren't all 'bad', I knew there were better and more aligned ways for me to make good money.

It's moments like those when we wake up. Truly wake up. There isn't always one single big awakening. Rather, it's lots of small ones. I'm constantly navigating and checking back in on decisions I've made to see whether they're still right for me. From the projects I work on to clients I work with, through to smaller decisions like what I put on social media each day.

Keep asking: *Is this in alignment with my soul? Is this an authentic expression of my beliefs and purpose, or is this simply about getting more likes?* You will never be everything to everybody, but you can be something special to your people. Speak for them, sing for them, and your success will feel so much sweeter.

Aligning and realigning your outer world with your inner world, your soul with your surroundings, is an ongoing practice. You will know when it feels 'off' or feels wrong.

For me, I feel either anxious or get an 'off' feeling in my tummy. Or I just feel really flat. You'll have your own way of knowing, so keep checking in to see if each project feels aligned.

COURAGE TO CHANGE

> I hope everyone that is reading this is having a really good day. And if you are not, just know that in every new minute that passes you have an opportunity to change that.
>
> – **Gillian Anderson**

Soulpreneurs frequently find themselves at a crossroad. As our soul and internal world expands and evolves at a rapid pace, we find ourselves looking around at our life and finding that it no longer aligns. There is a balance between gratitude, contentment and happiness with our life and continually wanting to check back in and create a life that mirrors our desires and dreams.

The biggest change for me was back when I transitioned from the music industry to the wellness world. At that time, my husband and I sold everything we had, including our prized Sydney beachside apartment, to create financial space for me to 'start from scratch' again, as a student of the wellbeing world. I left my career, my friends, my family and most of my belongings behind. I left behind the city that I had lived in and loved my whole life. I left it for dust. Nothing felt like it was in alignment with who I was becoming. I found myself constantly scribbling the words of the title of my favourite Juliana Hatfield album, *Become What You Are.*

Like all big change, it wasn't easy. For the first six months, I cried several times a week on the phone to my mama back in Sydney and wondered if it was the wrong decision. The only parts of my old life that remained with me were my beloved husband and my cats.

While I was scared of all the change, I was far more terrified of what would happen if things stayed the same. My body, heart and soul were loud and clear on this issue! My life needed to change, even though my head couldn't make sense of it at the time. I felt like I'd thrown away everything that I'd worked my whole life to achieve.

This was when I developed my deepest faith.

After a year, it became easier. Now many years later, I know that it was an inevitable change that was part of my divine destiny, which needed to happen for my soul and new career and direction to flourish. A year in, I found myself surrounded by new like-minded friends, although the first twelve months were pretty lonely. Isac had effortlessly eased into a work transfer in Brisbane, the closest city, an hour's drive away, which meant I was alone for five days a week, in a place where I knew barely anyone.

Trying to find my way, new doctors, new yoga studios, new everything, I inevitably spent lots of time by myself, before we adopted our dogs. I walked up and down the famous long stretches of Gold Coast beaches, visualising the new life that I had been called to come and create. By myself.

On reflection, I'm grateful for that time of solitude before I found my feet and my soul sisters. That cocoon of change allowed me to connect with who I truly was. To get to know myself again, to understand what I wanted to do and create without the influence or interference of others. It also gave me the opportunity to dive deeper into my own spiritual practice, as well as health and yoga studies.

As the money started to dry up, I started freelancing part-time for a wellbeing PR agency and for my new friends who were successful bloggers, artists and business owners. Then on one fateful afternoon walk, I heard the words 'Earth Events' and that dream and vision was born. It was just over a year after I'd left Sydney. I believe I needed that year of cocooning for all the self-exploration, inner soul work and getting a little lost, in order to find myself again.

There are journals and journals of ideas—some wonderful and some terrible—that I created in that year. Roundabouts and circles of ideas, trying to find the definitive answer to what I was here to do, what I was here to create. Hundreds of different business ideas, careers. Did I want to be a health coach or a yoga teacher? A publicist or an event promoter? A crystal healer or a juice shop owner? It changed every day, which is a natural part of the journey. Thank goodness for journals!

My husband would come home from his long daily city commute to hear me declaring, 'I've got it! I'm going to open a health cafe' one day and 'I'm totally clear now, I'm meant to run yoga retreats' the next. Sound familiar? Bless his patience. Patience was crucial for me and it will be for you. Be patient with yourself during this time. Keep exploring what lights you up.

Many people in this world avoid change at all costs, preferring to stay safe. It's understandable. Yet, as Soulpreneurs, we must embrace change.

After three years of successfully running Earth Events, I had to embrace change once again, when I felt the call to focus on my work with Soulpreneurs. She called to me and called to me for years, until I finally couldn't ignore her. It was time to change once again, to let go of Earth Events, to move into Soulpreneurs. It was challenging but oh so worth it! And no doubt the day will come when it will be time for me to change again, to follow my next call. I feel like this will happen my whole life.

My soul's contract was complete with Earth Events. I had set out to create life-changing events in the health and spiritual space and when we wrapped up, we were reaching more people than ever before. Over 100 events and 40,000 attendees later, I felt that my soul contract was complete. The circle was closed.

The same will happen with my Soulpreneurs contract. We've done a lot together, yet there is still more to come. And then one day, change will come again.

> Know that change is always challenged! When you decide that you want to make a change, it is the way of the Universe to throw obstacles in our way. It is like we are being tested to see how serious we really are about what it is we have said. See it for what it is, don't get discouraged and always keep going.
>
> – Gala Darling

EMBRACE BOTH CHANGE AND CONSISTENCY

Most of my community who have been with me since the beginning of Earth Events know that everything I do is done with the intention of creating a healthier and happier world, whether that's through events, courses, podcasts or books.

Stay consistent with your core intention and your audience will stay with you.

When I announced that I was adding an essential oils arm to my business, I was terrified of losing the support and faith of my clients and customers. But I received so much love and excitement, as my community understood how it aligned with my deepest intentions, and that my core and consistent intentions of creating health and happiness were stronger than ever.

While I had previously been negative and sceptical about network marketing, I shared that I had now seen and experienced a beautiful side to it. I even created a popular podcast episode (*The new wave of network marketing*) to celebrate this evolution. I'm so glad I had the courage to change my mind, to let my beliefs evolve and my business flourish into its next incarnation of divine destiny.

Here's an email I received from one of my longstanding students and clients, who is a psychologist:

> *I know you found some decisions difficult but it is so clear that you are on the right path and flowing with ease! There's nothing better than that and it is admirable. I have always admired your courage to aim high and to act on your vision. Changing our minds is not a sign of indecision, but rather a sign of openness and willingness to try new things and to find our bliss. Keep following your intuition, no matter what else is happening around you, and you can't go wrong. It's how I live my life too.*

When you think about change, what holds you back? What is stopping you?

We live in a world where many people continue on a path that was chosen for them, or one that they once chose for themselves but no longer aligns with their joy, their soul. The way you live your life is the greatest lesson you can teach others. Lead by example. Give others the confidence to change what is no longer working in their lives. Be the inspiration! Be the one who takes the risk. Security and safety are important, but not at the sacrifice of your soul.

While making major life or career changes can be terrifying, always remember there is something worse: regret! What could be worse than living with the fear and regret that you didn't take the risk? Seize the day and make the change.

It's a philosophy of life. A practice. If you do this, something will change; what will change is that you will change, your life will change, and if you can change you, you can perhaps change the world.

– **Vivienne Westwood**

TRANSFORMING COMPARISON INTO CELEBRATION

Comparison is the thief of joy.

– **Theodore Roosevelt**

Two of the biggest Soulpreneur dream killers are comparison and competition. From the music industry through to the wellness world, I've seen comparison rob even the most successful people of their peace and divine path.

It never ends. The more successful you get, the more you will compare yourself to others you perceive as further ahead than you ... and there will always be someone ahead. Dissolving these self-destructive patterns early on will save you a whole lot of pain in the long run.

Social media has become a hotbed of comparisonitis, as we see the highlight reels of others while we are in our darkest moments. They highlight the failures or inadequacies we are feeling in our own life and just how 'not enough' we are. This makes us miserable, bitter and resentful towards our peers and so-called competitors and also towards ourselves, for not being far enough, ahead enough, loved enough.

Comparison fuels our ego and sabotages our soul. Yet what if we could admire the success of others as inspiration of what's possible for us? What if we could celebrate the success of others without feeling that we are less than them? What if we could honour our different stages, paces and journeys?

While the feeling of comparison or competition may never entirely go away, you have a choice of whether to act on it.

An alternative is to step back and deep breathe. Then call it for what it is: 'Oh hello comparisonitis, I see you there ... how interesting.' Let him have his moment to direct your attention to a part of yourself that is feeling inadequate or unloved.

Comparing ignites an energy of lack and scarcity, which we can transform back to abundant and expansive energy by first cracking out a fresh gratitude list! Instead of allowing comparison to put all of our focus onto what others appear to have, let's switch focus to what you have.

Your circumstances, gifts and path are far too unique to compare to others. It's simply unfair on yourself and others. We never know what's really happening behind the scenes, how many hours, weeks, months or years they've put in, what sacrifices were made, or the challenges happening behind the social media screens.

In Iyanla Vanzant's words: *Comparison is the act of violence against the self.*

When we compete against others, we are competing against our true selves. Instead of focusing and flowing on our soul's journey and divine timing, we become driven by external forces outside of ourselves: the people we consider our competitors.

This is when we make decisions that are not aligned with our soul's purpose and path, and we speed up at times when we need to slow down. It's when we make head-driven, forceful, clingy and desperate grabs to things and timings that were never destined to be ours. That don't fulfil or serve us.

We somehow compare our goals, achievements and lives to those that our soul never really wanted to be or have in the first place; we step out of our own lane and run someone else's race. Not only is it a train wreck waiting to happen, it's an icky push and hustle the whole way to a destination we never wanted to arrive at in the first place.

Remember, there is only one person that we can aim to be better than: the person we were yesterday.

Stay in your lane

Run your own race

Celebrate the success of others and always remember that there is more than enough for all of us

> A flower does not think of competing to
> the flower next to it. It just blooms.
>
> – Zen Shin

SOULPRENEUR STEPS

Step away from your social media and open up your journal, copying these words and filling in the blanks:

How interesting that ________________________ has achieved/received ________________________ which makes me feel ________________________ which I want to celebrate for them, although for now I'm going to take time out doing ________________________ and remembering there is more than enough for all of us. I'm grateful they have shown me what is possible. I am also grateful for ________________________.

Now list three people you currently compare yourself to and why:

....

....

....

Are they helping you identify a part of your own business or life that needs attention?

Are they distracting you from your real work in the world?

Are these people you can celebrate or collaborate with?

~ SOULPRENEUR SUCCESS SUMMARY ~

✓ *Journal out your limiting beliefs.*

✓ *Reframe negative thoughts into a helpful procrastination-busting mindset.*

✓ *Put in place confidence-boosting rituals.*

✓ *Reaffirm your core intentions.*

✓ *Get support and healing to help you in times where you need courage, persistence and patience.*

✓ *Celebrate your peers and explore collaborative opportunities with them.*

chapter NINE

The Path to Abundance and Prosperity

Abundance is not something we acquire.
It is something we tune into.

– Wayne Dyer

FROM SCARCITY TO ABUNDANCE MINDSET

While writing out my mission for the year on a bright and sparkly new year's day, it became crystal clear to me: *I am here to get more money into the hands of healers and creatives.*

Can you imagine a world where more people like you, me and your fellow Soulpreneurs have the majority of money, power, influence and affluence? I believe it would be a pretty beautiful place and certainly a step in the right direction.

We have a fair bit of work to do to bring this vision and dream to life, because there's still that old-school 'starving artist' stereotype and the false belief that 'money isn't spiritual' floating around. There is a scarcity mindset that doesn't serve us, or the people and planet that we care so much about.

In this chapter, we'll turn the focus back on creating a bank balance that sets up your business with bricks not sticks, to help you come from a place of abundant service rather than scarcity. Because it's so challenging to be in your true purpose and potential, contributing and making your full impact in the world, if you're scratching away trying to pay the bills.

When you feel financially stable, that feeds your basic needs of security, food and shelter, setting up the whole vibration and energy of your business.

Looking back at our chakras, we can see that the soul of our business needs its base chakra nourished before we can move into our creative, giving and spiritual chakras. Our first chakra, our base chakra, is our food, shelter, security and grounding. It's nourishing food and a roof over our heads—basic survival needs including the grocery bills and the mortgage. The foundation on which we build our lives.

An unstable or blocked base chakra in our business will lead to chronic anxiety, stress, negativity and living in fear. This will lead to making poor decisions, out of alignment with our soul's purpose.

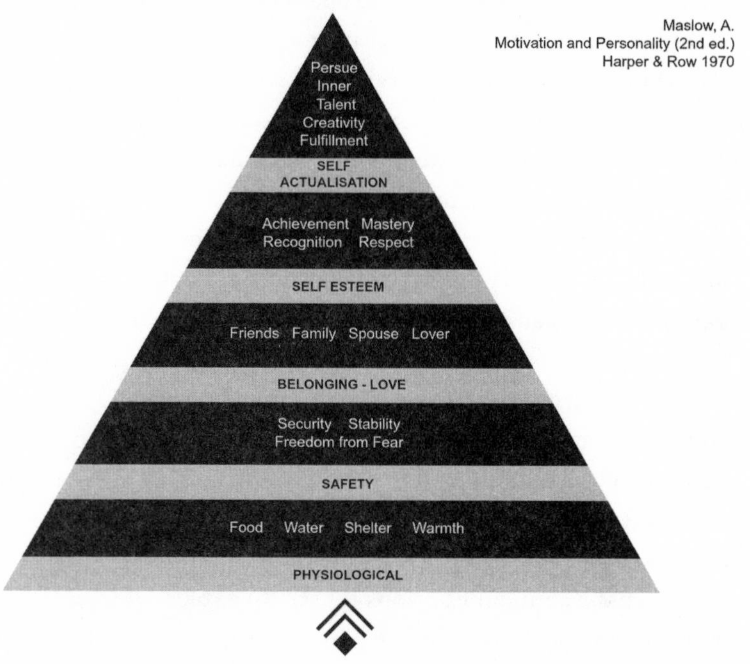

Fear and scarcity rarely lead us to soul-fulfilling decisions. We are in survival mode, not soul-fulfilment mode. A lack of money will lead us away from our mission whereas, when our base chakra is rock solid, our mission aligns with our soul (which is not a mission to make money).

This is one of many reasons why I encourage you to keep some form of financial nourishment other than your business while starting this work, at least until the income is steady and somewhat effortless. Yes, this often means keeping your day job or other forms of stable income, until your soul work starts to receive a steady financial stream.

Sometimes this may even mean returning to a part-time day job temporarily to help you build up that foundation again, while you prepare and plan for your next soul venture. There is no shame in this. It's not a backward step, so never be embarrassed. It's a sign of even higher devotion to your soul work that you want to do it in a slow, steady and sustainable way, instead of just jumping at a quick buck.

I do not believe that we can all take a 'leap of faith' in leaving our financial stability to start a business from scratch. Many of us have mortgages and children to take into account, or no savings or safety net to fall back on.

Be real with yourself and your financial position. Ease into your new income from your soul work. Make it a smooth and sustainable transition. Explore income streams that are not your soul work exactly, but are certainly in alignment with it. We talk about affiliate sponsorships and network marketing later, and these may be abundant options for you to explore.

Before we get to that, let's explore any caps, barriers and glass ceilings to what you believe is possible, because abundance starts in your mind well before it appears in your bank account. Let's dig into your relationship with money now, and open up to the abundance that is your birthright.

SOULPRENEUR STEPS

Start with gratitude and **count your blessings** for all you have by answering these questions on the lines below or in your journal:

> *What are the income streams or money in your life now?*
> *Do you feel that hard work is the only way to receive money?*

> *How do you feel about accepting money for doing something you love?*
> *How do you feel about receiving money from unwell people for healing work?*
> *How do you feel about putting a price tag on your creative work?*

The greatest discovery of all time is that a person can change his future by merely changing his attitude.

– Oprah Winfrey

RECEIVING AND VALUING YOUR WORTH

Many of us only feel comfortable receiving abundance for work or activities that feel hard or unenjoyable. Or we feel guilty charging people who are experiencing challenges. I've seen this over the years with healers who don't want to charge clients with cancer or life-threatening conditions, even though their work is of such high value and contribution that their clients are thrilled to pay for the healing they have received.

The Universe gave healers these great gifts with the intention that they share and sustain themselves financially through them. You were not born with your healing or creative gifts to simply throw them aside to go make a living doing something completely unaligned. Your angels want you to create abundance with the gifts you were given. Stop sitting on them, hiding them away or undercharging for them.

Years ago when I was first diagnosed with cancer, I was so grateful for the wonderful healers and helpers in my life that I would have paid ten times more than they charged me! They were worth every cent and, on reflection, they were undercharging me.

And it's not just about attracting the money in the first place. It's about what we do with it once it comes in, since Soulpreneurs can feel uneasy with money in their hands or bank accounts.

Let's explore your **beliefs about money** right now, so we can overcome this mindset.

> *Do you believe you are 'good' or 'bad' with money?*
> *What are your past experiences with money?*

- *How do you feel about spending money on others rather than on yourself?*
- *Are there money mistakes, losses or experiences that need forgiveness (of self or others)?*
- *What is your current financial position? Do you feel in lack, secure or abundant?*
- *Who is responsible for your current financial position and feelings?*
- *What are your parents' experiences and conversations around money and success?*
- *Did you hear any of the following growing up?* Money doesn't grow on trees. Money is the root of all evil or greed. Work isn't for enjoyment.
- *What was the language in your home around money?*
- *Did your parents argue about money?*
- *What is your earliest money memory?*
- *If you received an allowance or pocket money, what was the energy around that?*
- *Were you trusted to be responsible and make your own money decisions?*
- *What are your partner's/friends' experiences and conversations around money and success?*
- *What will everyone think and say if you start being 'seen' as successful?*
- *What would change if you become the wealthiest person you know?*
- *What do you believe are the limits of money or success that are available to you?*

Your relationship with money is more sacred and spiritual than you may give it credit for. Think of financials of your business as the lungs, inhaling and exhaling oxygen and life through your business, allowing you to grow, serve and sustain yourself in the long run.

Money is a wonderful energy exchange between you and your audience, and between you and the people working in your business. Allow this flow of finance.

Part of this is about investing money for your business to operate, but you also need to feel confident in charging, accepting and receiving money, which can be a challenge when you have limiting beliefs. However, it's valuable to remember the positive side of what money gives us.

SOULPRENEUR STEPS

Set your **intentions around money** here. Why would money want to land in your hands? How will you treat her? What will you and money co-create together?

What are three to five words that describe how you feel about money?

....

....

....

....

....

What difference will more money make to your:

Family

....

....

Physical health

....

....

Mental wellbeing

....

....

Business

....

....

Audience, clients and community

....

....

Causes and charities

....

....

See how many others will be blessed by your abundance!

FINANCIAL FREEDOM

What does financial freedom mean to you? Travel, regular holidays, fancy cars, big houses, designer clothes? To me, financial freedom is about:

> *The freedom from worrying about money.*
> *The freedom to live where I want to live.*
> *The freedom to wake up when I want, wear whatever I want and go wherever I want.*
> *The freedom to spend all day creating or connecting, from a place of joy and love.*
> *The freedom from feeling like I have to do something just for money.*
> *The freedom to donate and contribute to all the charities and causes I believe in.*

This kind of freedom lets my soul fly wild and free, expressing what she wants, when she chooses. To feel like she is making a difference and positive contributions where needed.

The funny thing is that financial freedom has never meant cars, boats or travel to me—not that there's anything wrong with those desires. If your dream is to travel or buy a houseboat, then add that to your goals and vision board right now. Let's make that dream a reality.

Your financial freedom dream must resonate with you. It must set your soul on fire.

THE ART OF RECEIVING

Soulpreneurs tend to be generous givers. We have that down pat. Yet when it comes to receiving—money, help or even a compliment—many of us haven't developed a sense of feeling comfortable to receive, either not believing we deserve to receive, or that we are worthy, or even that we are here to receive.

Those old feelings of unworthiness or 'not good enough' rise. We question our self-worth. Others of us have developed a belief that giving is far more soulful or spiritually superior to receiving. We forget we are equally important.

Here's the truth: **the more we receive, the more we have to give**.

Please accept this as your permission slip to start receiving—money, help, compliments, assistance—because the more you fill your cup, the more you can pour into others. The more money flowing into your bank account, the more you can donate or contribute to others. This is about equal exchange.

SOULPRENEUR STEPS

It's time to **make a declaration** and claim that you are **worthy to receive**. Fill in the blank and read this aloud:

> *I, ______________________________ am allowed to ask for and graciously accept an abundance of money for doing what I love in the world. I welcome all help, assistance and compliments that come my way. I am ready and open to receive all that the world wishes to give me. I am worthy and I deserve a life of limitless abundance. I am more than good enough.*

THE STARVING ARTIST MINDSET

Oh, the 90s hangover of the 'anti sell-out' movement! I'm certainly not here to tell you to sell yourself out or sacrifice what is true to your soul. That ain't the Soulpreneur style. But please let's drop the glorification of the struggling or starving artist. Those images have been painted for us since the 18th century, right back to the *La Bohème* opera.

The stereotype spills into the world of creatives and healers today. We still see these noble archetypes working their wonders and healing lives, yet they can't pay their own rent.

Few issues fire me up quite like this, as it breaks my heart to see my favourite healers and creatives struggling financially. I want to see them (you!) making awesome money and taking care of themselves, continuing to create and heal and share their soul work with the world for generations to come.

Will you join the revolution? Sustainability, longevity, refusing to choose between making money and doing your soul work—I believe you can have them all!

SOULPRENEUR STEPS

Affirmations are **positive statements** that we repeat aloud, or write down in a place we will see regularly, like the car, the bathroom mirror, the fridge. These positive statements help affirm our new beliefs.

Create or choose your new **money mantras**. Lock in your new expansive beliefs by reciting the affirmations that match the mindset you need. Write some of your own (on Post-It notes) or borrow mine:

> *I am a Soulpreneur.*
> *I create success that feels good on the inside.*

- *I let my soul lead the way.*
- *I am ready for my divine destiny.*
- *I am ready to receive money for work that feels easy.*
- *I love and approve of myself.*
- *I forgive myself and others for past mistakes.*
- *I am a wiser person and teacher, because of my past mistakes.*
- *I am protected by a higher source.*
- *I am loved and lovable.*
- *Everything is happening in divine timing.*
- *I am open to seeing the good in every situation.*
- *I am organised.*
- *My work day is peaceful and productive.*
- *I allow creativity to flow through me.*
- *I allow myself to be seen as imperfect.*
- *I am ready to receive divine abundance.*
- *I am open to seeing and following the signs that lead to abundance through my purpose.*
- *I am already getting wealthier.*
- *I love using my unique gifts and experiences to help people.*
- *I always do my best, honouring when it is time to rise and when it is time to rest.*
- *I allow myself time and space to recharge.*
- *I am unaffected by what others say or think about me.*
- *I am gracious in receiving and generous in giving.*
- *I am ready for the next step.*
- *I express myself with compassion and confidence.*
- *I am ready to become the wealthiest person I know.*
- *I welcome in positive change.*
- *I am clear, confident and courageous.*
- *I allow old relationships to dissolve with love.*
- *I find compassion and forgiveness easily.*

- *I am kind and forgiving to myself.*
- *My biggest obstacles are my biggest lessons.*
- *I heal the world through healing myself.*
- *I am okay with not everyone understanding my work in the world.*
- *I am the creator of my own life.*
- *I am not the same person I was yesterday.*
- *I trust myself with money.*
- *I have faith in myself.*
- *I am excited to help people with my wealth.*
- *I always have more than enough money to pay my bills with ease.*
- *I take a positive and proactive approach to managing my bank accounts.*
- *I am thankful to pay big tax bills.*
- *I am aligned with my true purpose.*
- *I love investing into my business and career.*
- *I experience love wherever I go.*
- *I am actively aware of how much is flowing in and out of my bank account.*
- *I love maintaining a surplus of money in my account.*
- *My sensitivity is my magic.*
- *I honour my body and soul with nourishing foods and words.*
- *I dissolve old stories that no longer serve me.*
- *It is safe for me to say 'no' to things that do not light me up.*
- *It is safe for me to change my mind.*
- *I allow my soul to soar.*
- *I am exactly where I am meant to be in this moment.*
- *My self-love and self-respect inspire those around me.*
- *My success inspires those around me.*
- *I make smart decisions that serve me and my audience.*
- *I am more than good enough.*
- *I am more than beautiful enough.*

> *I am more than wise enough.*
> *I believe in community and collaboration.*
> *I am free-flowing and flexible.*
> *I always find my way back on track.*
> *My vision creates my world.*
> *I am a magnet for miracles and money.*
> *The past is the past and has no power in my present or future.*
> *I trust my instincts.*
> *I have faith to follow my gut feeling.*
> *I love taking care of my mind, body and soul.*
> *I am excellent at finding solutions to any challenge or obstacle.*
> *I ask for help and accept support.*
> *I am doing work that fulfils my soul.*
> *I love learning about how business financials thrive.*
> *I love money and money loves me.*
> *I am deeply fulfilled by my work in the world.*
> *I love the people I work with.*
> *I love the audience I serve.*
> *I take action and invest in my future abundance.*
> *I am worthy of success.*
> *I am worthy of being seen and admired.*
> *I am worthy of being inspiring.*
> *I am worthy of doing work I love.*
> *Abundance is my birthright.*

You can download an affirmations audio I've created for you here: www.yvetteluciano.com/bookclub

A SOULFUL APPROACH TO SELLING

What if I told you that you never needed to sell a single thing to have a successful business? Obviously that's almost impossible, as sales corresponds to income and can define the difference between a hobby and a business. But what if I told you there was a way to sell that **felt** like you weren't actually selling anything? And that sales and income would roll in regardless.

This is how I feel almost every day. Even with sales flowing in, I don't feel like I'm selling. I'm **sharing**.

Sharing excitement about courses I've created that I believe will change careers and lives.

Sharing and inviting people to events that will be transformational experiences for all who attend.

Sharing my obsession with essential oils that have brought me deeper peace and purpose.

Sharing music or art that lifts spirits and heals hearts.

Sharing anything I feel will help others, ensuring they know where to find the solutions to their challenges and answers to their prayers.

We don't sell products or services. We sell solutions to problems. And I'm in love with helping solve people's problems.

Soulpreneurs don't need to use sleazy sales tricks or tactics. We simply need to share the products and services that we love with authenticity by communicating:

- *Why we created the offering*
- *Why we stand by the offering (if it's another company's or person's product)*
- *How it's changing lives (ours and others), where personal stories are key to soulful selling*
- *What makes it so special or unique to other offerings (without bagging out others)*
- *Who the offering is specifically for (and why it was created with them in mind)*

> *How it all works and how to purchase*

This last one may sound obvious, but remember that confused customers will not buy. The steps to buy or sign up must be simple and straightforward.

People love to buy products and services that will improve their lives. Most people love shopping! And yet they don't like the feeling of being sold to. Yes, they can **feel** it.

SOULPRENEUR STEPS

If you want to feel more comfortable selling, work through these questions:

> *What are the first three words that you associate with the word 'selling'?*
> *What negative experiences have you had as a buyer?*
> *What positive experiences have you enjoyed as a buyer?*
> *What shopping experiences do you enjoy and why?*

List out the last ten products or services you purchased (check your bank if you need to). What inspired you to buy them, and what was the buying experience like? Did you have hesitations and, if so, why and how did you move through them?

1. ....

2. ....

3. ....

4. ....

5. ....

6. ....

7. ....

8. ....

9. ....

10. ....

When you think about selling products and services, do any of the following concerns come to mind? Please circle any that are relevant to you:

> *Fear of rejection*
> *Fear of failure*
> *Fear of being judged*
> *Fear of being seen as 'pushy'*
> *Guilt when charging for your products or services*

When someone declines your offering, it's not personal; it's about them and where they are at. Sometimes it might not be a 'no,' sometimes it's a 'not now.'

THE SELLING/SHARING/BUYING EXPERIENCE

As Soulpreneurs, we have the opportunity to create soulful selling experiences. I love to create opportunities for new clients or customers to 'try before they buy' with money-back guarantees on my courses. With my essential oils, I enjoy engaging their senses by smelling and touching the oils in a class or through samples.

Humans love to engage their senses, seeing, hearing, touching, tasting or smelling before buying. This is one of the coolest aspects to the new wave of direct selling. It's done in people's homes or on personal calls with them, and is far less 'home party' style and more educational. I host mine in soul sister circle style.

Your customers, clients and audience will believe and buy into your vibe. They know when you're being authentically enthusiastic about what you're offering. They feel when it's the real deal, especially if they're smart cookies or empaths themselves.

So instead of focusing on the 'selling' word, focus on **touching their soul**.

Lastly, but most importantly, **listen up**! Selling is more about listening than speaking. It's about hearing and understanding the problems or challenges that your audience is facing, connecting on a soul level and providing them with the solution. This is the feminine style, because we want to help, soothe and support.

People don't buy things. They buy solutions to their problems. Maybe we buy lavender to help us sleep, jewellery to express our values and identity, flights to get our toes in the sand.

Focus on the benefits and the outcome rather than the item, the thing that you're selling.

The non-negotiable in soulful selling is that it must be a product or service that aligns with your soul, that you **know** must be shared with the world, shared with your audience. Whether it's something you have written or performed, or something that you have the opportunity to get in the hands of your audience made by someone else, an event ticket, coaching session or enrolment to one of the courses you create, the same principles apply. It all comes down to being deeply grateful for the tools being in your life, and how deeply needed you know they are in the wider community.

For me, devotion to an event made me want everyone to come to it. Devotion to essential oils made me want to place natural solutions in as many hands and homes as possible.

We need to remember that we are not selling useless, soulless products or services here. Remove the stereotype of a sleazy car salesman trying to rip people off by selling dodgy cars. We are getting music, art and healing into the hands of those who need it!

It's almost funny that Soulpreneurs are the ones who most shy away from selling, yet we are the ones who are sharing and selling what will most heal the world. There is no sense in that. It's kinda insane actually. So, let's be loud and proud. Let's honour that these products and services chose us to be the ones to share them with the world.

If you flip over and look at it from the customer's point of view, aren't you so grateful to the healers who sold you sessions, music promoters who sold you concert tickets, your bestie who sold you essential oils and the store who sold you your yoga mat? I know I am! Thankfully, they didn't shy away from sharing their offerings with me.

And that's what it comes down to in the end. These words, work, music, messages, art, products, gifts of Mama Earth—they chose **you** to be their guardian and custodian, the one who gets to share and sell them to the world. Honour this mission, Soulpreneur! Graciously accept.

Let people buy your vibe. They are drawn to you for a reason. They buy emotionally, energetically. They buy with their heart.

Ask yourself how you and your offer are going to help them. Imagine how it will improve their lives. Listen to their challenges and concerns, then place a specific **needed** solution right in their hands.

That, my sweetheart, is soulful selling.

ENOUGH FOR EVERYONE

The news and media thrives on telling us that there is not enough, that we are lacking and that we are in fear. Not enough jobs, never enough money.

Considering that we have grown up having these messages blared into our sensitive ears over TV or radio programs, it's no wonder we believe everything is a race and there is only enough for the elite few or those in first place. That the only way to ever become wealthy, abundant and affluent is to be born on the right side of the tracks, or to claw your way up the scarcity food chain.

What if we grew up being told that we live in an abundant Universe, rather than one of scarcity? That there is no 'us and them'? That abundance and prosperity were not reserved for an elite few?

What if money **did** grow on trees? What if we could all tune in to the frequency of financial abundance? What if we could all tap into the vibration of prosperity?

Self-made millionaire Tara Bliss is one of my beloved business collaborators and best friends. I say she is 'self-made' but Tara might well say that it was all in collaboration with her team and spiritual guides. When we first met, she was starting her first business from a hot and sweaty tiny bedroom in her mother's house in Brisbane. Fast forward five years and we were celebrating Tara becoming a self-made millionaire in the same year she turned thirty!

Tara's dedication to being of highest service to her community has continued to grow. Her devotion to leading with love and light has not wavered. What has changed though is her money mindset and rituals. Tara believes that money may not be able to speak, but money is listening to everything we say about it in every moment.

Money knows how often people are complaining, blaming, resisting, pretending they don't want, need and love it, when in actual fact they do.

SOULPRENEUR STEPS

One of Tara's personal rituals, which we can action immediately, is writing letters to the Bank of the Universe. You may wish to borrow hers and customise it or write your own personal money magic letter.

Dear Bank of the Universe

Thank you for providing me with all the resources, opportunities and financial abundance I need to create the most appropriate impact on the lives of myself, my family and those I serve. Thank you for knowing that you are safe with me.

Thank you for giving me the opportunity for world class mentoring by the one and only [insert dream mentor here]. I have always wanted to work with her and now, because of you, I can. What she teaches me directly impacts my community, and I feel honoured and deeply humbled to be held in the hands of the best there is.

Thank you for making it possible for me to continually invest in my growth: programs, events, books, masterminds. Thank you for flowing freely to us through the spirit of [insert your business/project/art/expression here], so that we may make whatever decisions are in the highest good for her, her staff and her customers.

Thank you for entering my energy field so that I may continue to invest into [insert your business/project/art/expression here], travelling and teaching and passing on the same lessons that you have been teaching me. My wealth grows to the extent in which I grow myself. Because of you, I'm able to encourage so many others to step fully into their own growth path and rewrite the money story of their whole family.

Thank you for allowing me to step away from the things that don't feel in alignment with me and thus dilute my impact and message. You allow me to hire, delegate, shuffle, reassess and reprioritise constantly.

Thank you for the opportunity to live a life of wild adventure, play and memory-making. The travel that you bestow upon me, the beautiful dinners, the spontaneous road trips, the outrageous ways I'm now able to give to those I love … I am forever grateful.

Thank you for circulating so perfectly in and out of me, in a way that is just as it should be. As I sit here and humbly ask for more, I can feel your trust in my request. And I know, with every cell in my body, that it is coming.

All my love, Tara xo

Write your own letter to the Bank of the Universe here:

....

....

....

....

....

....

....

....

....

~ SOULPRENEUR SUCCESS SUMMARY ~

✓ *Get clear on your value.*

✓ *Explore your memories and belief system around money.*

✓ *Know why you're making money and what financial freedom will enable you to do.*

✓ *Surround yourself with the right tools and mantras for a positive money mindset.*

✓ *Reframe selling for yourself—no more starving artist!*

✓ *Clarify the problems you want to solve for your clients or customers.*

✓ *Write your letter to the Bank of the Universe.*

chapter TEN

Shining in Your Sensitivity

As we let our own light shine, we unconsciously give other people permission to do the same. As we are liberated from our own fear, our presence automatically liberates others.
— **Marianne Williamson,** ***A Return to Love***

STEPPING INTO YOUR SPOTLIGHT

Time to explore **why** you wish to be seen and heard. We know our ego desires fame and attention. Yet our soul wishes to serve.

How do we feel the difference? Your ego will focus on being seen and heard for validation, celebrity or superiority. Whereas your soul will deeply desire to reach and connect with more people to help them, to serve them.

Your ego will be the confusing trickster who focuses your attention on fame for fame's sake, yet will be in your ear telling you that you are not worthy to be seen and heard: *Who are you to step into the spotlight?*

Clarity around why you wish to be heard will keep you aligned when you want to hide away, or are crossing the ego line.

SOULPRENEUR STEPS

Ask yourself: ***Who do I wish to see and hear me?*** Check back in on the wishes you held for your audience in Chapter 7. They are who you need to focus on. This isn't actually about you. This is about your people, your community, the souls who need to hear and see you.

....

....

....

....

....

Next ask: ***How will I be seen and heard?*** Check back on your Truth Trifecta natural talents from Chapter 1. Whether it be writing, blogging, books, speaking or videos, choose to share your soul work through a platform that aligns with your talents and is easily accessible to your audience.

....

....

....

....

....

Then look at: ***When and what do I want to share?*** How much and how soon to share a story is a personal decision for each individual Soulpreneur. However, I would recommend being mindful to not share deeply delicate stories when you are in the eye of the storm. Write, journal, record about them privately. Wait to share the wisdom once the storm has passed.

Retrospect is a wonderful tool, and it's important not only to protect ourselves, but also the others in our lives who are part of the story, and the audience who are reading, watching and listening.

Some of us move through muddy patches more quickly than others. Respect your pace. If your stories are traumatic or heartbreaking, receive plenty of private healing and counselling before sharing publicly. Your audience members are not your therapists. They are not there to hold space for you as you share emotional stories. Your audience is there to receive your lessons and golden nuggets.

SHARING PERSONAL STORIES

Sharing personal stories is a significant part of being a transformational speaker, author and teacher. The key here is the word 'transformation.' If you are still the caterpillar or in the cocoon, it's your time for private processing and healing. When you start to break through as the beautiful butterfly, it's your time to shine and share your experience and what you've learnt from it. That doesn't mean you can't share other inspiring stories while in the cocoon, so continue to share and speak about other things. **Other** things.

When my surrogacy journey started, I decided I was ready to share more about my cancer journey which had started many years earlier. It was time. My surrogacy journey? It's too soon to share publicly; I'm still in the thick of it.

The difference is my cancer stories or business journeys feel safer to share now that I've had space and reflection time. When I was in the cocoon around cancer or a business lesson, that didn't mean I had to stop everything altogether. I had a backlog of abundant lessons to share and speak on. I'm sure you do too.

You may choose to not be as selective or protective as I am. Like all Soulpreneur decisions, we need to make the best decision for our own personal path. The details you share come down to two questions:

- *What are you ready to share?*
- *What is the intention of your sharing?*

Consider the details that are **required** to engage your audience and ignite the desired emotion. For instance, when I'm sharing my cancer journey at National Breast Cancer Foundation fundraisers, I share the specific details and stories that ignite empathy and inspiration. I desire for the audience to understand how unexpected this cancer was and that it can happen to anyone; how devastating it felt to receive that diagnosis; then how uplifting it was to know there were so many treatment options available for me, with research continuing for the thousands of other women like me.

The intention of that talk is to help the audience feel proud of their donations and contributions, to know how grateful I and my fellow thrivers are, and to inspire them to continue making a difference by donating and supporting more research. I also do these talks with the intention of giving hope to my fellow cancer thrivers.

I do not go too deeply into the gruesome details of my cancer story on stage or on camera. That is for my private healing sessions, friends and family. That has been my choice up to this stage. It may change in the future. (Yes, you're allowed to change your mind as many times as you want!) For now, that's what feels good.

What and when you choose to share should be greatly influenced by **intention**, always taking responsibility for the stories and energy you put out into the world. Especially when your audience has sensitive souls too.

RESPECTING PRIVACY

When our stories involve others, it adds an extra layer of sensitivity, in particular when it includes clients or children. Below I've suggested some steps you can take.

Clients

- Ask your client's written approval before sharing any stories or case studies, even if you think they are positive and uplifting. There is a moral code and, in many states and countries, there are legal requirements.
- Even if you have received your client's approval, sharing a story or case study may scare other potential clients away from sharing vulnerably with you, if they think they might end up being in your work down the track. You can mitigate against this by making it clear that the words are only shared with permission, and by writing a confidentiality policy that you make publicly available for your potential clients.

Children

- Hold off sharing specific stories and details about children until they are adults.
- Even if the parent of the child has approved you using a story, be respectful that the child may not be thrilled about that decision in the future.
- When sharing about your own journey as a parent, focus more on the details of your experience rather than the child's. Expressing **your** feelings about the rite of passage of your daughter starting school is wonderful, but different to sharing the details of your daughter's day. Share about **your** experience as a parent, not **their** experiences as a child. Another option is to change names, locations, ages and gender significantly when sharing these stories.

While these guidelines may seem extreme, we are still early on in the big picture of social media and online etiquette, not to mention laws governing this space, so we cannot be entirely aware of future repercussions regarding privacy issues.

The same guidelines apply to family and friends. In a time when we are overexposed to each other's stories and personal lives, we need to be mindful of the increased lack of privacy. Open up a conversation with your loved ones about how they feel about the possibility of you sharing about them.

I have family and friends who support and love the work I do in the world; however, they do not wish to be mentioned in my stories or be on my Instagram. They have chosen a different and private life for themselves, a decision I respect deeply, especially when it involves their children.

FAME

As Soulpreneurs, we aren't as pulled by fame as others may be, but it can creep in. When it does, we lose track of **why** we are doing what we're doing. And we get caught in the trap of seeking to impress and gain 'followers' rather than being of true service to others, our audience, our people.

You don't need thousands and thousands of random followers to sustain a successful business. Many of us could run abundant businesses with just a few hundred devoted customers or a handful of loyal clients!

Let's balance the conversation on stepping out into your spotlight (which I definitely want you to do!) with a reality check as you consider **why** you do what you do.

In Eckhart Tolle's book, *A New Earth,* he writes of fame being 'the ego's strategy of gaining a superior identity and importance in the eyes of others.' Tolle speaks of his growing concern regarding famous people falling for the image people and the media have created of them, and the line that is crossed when they begin to actually see themselves as superior to ordinary mortals. As a result, they sadly become increasingly disconnected and alienated from their true selves and others. As they become more dependent on their continuing popularity, they become unhappier and incapable of genuine relationships with anyone, including themselves, choosing to only surround themselves with others who feed their inflated self-image.

Social media stars have spoken about their struggle with clarity on who they really are behind their highlight reels and feeds. Always performing, always on show, always on brand, on trend and 'liked.'

As Soulpreneurs, we need to remind ourselves to stay grounded and focused on being of service.

THE PATH TO WISDOM

> There is scarcely any passion without struggle.
>
> – Albert Camus

Our Universe, our angels, our guides—they all conspire to help us on the path to our highest good. This path isn't always rainbows and unicorns. It can be dark, lonely and frightening at times. Some of the world's greatest teachers didn't come from a background of university degrees or online courses. They were born through life experiences and lessons.

While I don't wish trauma or crisis on anyone, I do believe that the lessons learnt—the light we find in our darkest night—are the gold we were born to share. Because we were strong enough to make it through, resilient enough to get back up, and wise enough to know this lesson needs to be shared. There is a spiritual growth and inheritance that can only be received, deeply understood and interpreted in those moments—the moments when we are crying in the car, curled up in a ball on the floor or petrified in a doctor's office.

Through the pain comes an awareness and longing for a higher purpose than we've ever experienced. A determination to help others in that exact moment, in that exact pain. Our empathy is born, our compassion is deepened and our devotion to preventing others feeling that way is fierce.

'Always darkest before the dawn' is a phrase and lyric you will be familiar with for good reason.

I don't mean to hope that we manifest more dark times. What I'm saying is that, when they do inevitably arrive, we need to be open to receiving the lessons. Every time there is a soul challenge in my life, I'm known to say: 'I wonder what lessons are coming through this?'

While you don't need to go that far, I encourage you to be present with the pain. Honour the process. Pay attention to how you feel and get all the help you need. Don't try to analyse your way through it or let anyone else 'strategy coach' you through your trauma. Feel it, cry it, scream it and be in it.

As my dear friend, actress and author Charlotte Carr, loves to remind me in these moments: 'It's too early to be shitting rainbows.'

Yes, there is meaning and teaching that will come. Don't try to find it too early, or 'over-spiritualise' every little thing too soon. Trying to speed race through our pain not only leads to ongoing struggles with inner peace but we miss the lessons and the light. As the great Leonard Cohen sang: *There's a crack in everything, that's how the light gets in.*

A part of me loves the darkness. I've come to peace with knowing that, at least a few times a year, I will disappear into a dark cocoon, usually triggered by a new life challenge or a memory or old wound being reopened. I'll pull away from everyday life, become my most introverted, listen to my favourite old dark music and journal a lot.

I've learnt to let myself be at peace with her, that Goth grunge teen, who just wants to write angst-filled stories and songs. She has a time and place. She makes me whole. Because how can I truly live in the light without having a shadow?

Without honouring her, I could not experience or understand the full spectrum of my emotions, nor empathise with others facing their own shadow. I appreciate that every time my darkness comes to visit, she ignites a reassessing, reincarnating, reawakening fire in my belly.

All of us experience a rebirth every time we move through a soul challenge—sometimes mini, sometimes massive. It doesn't matter whether that crisis is a diagnosis, divorce, death of a dream or a loved one; rebirth is inevitable.

> We must be willing to get rid of the life we've planned, so as to have the life that is waiting for us.
>
> – Joseph Campbell

DARK NIGHT OF THE SOUL

In the spiritual and personal development world, you may hear the term 'dark night of the soul'. We've adopted this term from religious origins: Roman Catholic Saint John of the Cross, who was well known for his writings and studies on the growth of the soul, described the dark night as a spiritual crisis in the journey towards union with God.

Nowadays, you will hear musicians, artists and authors from Depeche Mode to Stephen King reference the dark night of the soul. While definitions differ depending on the teacher or writer, a dark night of the soul is commonly defined or identified with any of the following:

- *Existential crisis*
- *Shattering of your sense of reality or world views*
- *Something once important to you feels meaningless*
- *Ego death*
- *Feeling a sense of being reborn*
- *Craving a clean slate of life and pondering the deepest, darkest questions, which makes small talk challenging*
- *Feeling alone in the world*
- *Feeling isolated and disconnected from others around you*

> *Awareness of your own mortality and the impermanence of everything*
> *Feeling like there is no choice about whether to make changes in your life*
> *Knowing you need more meaning, no matter how daunting the changes that must happen*

It's normal for these feelings to extend well past one night, lasting days, weeks, months. If you identify with the above feelings, do not go it alone. The help of a professional healer or psychologist will greatly support you. They will help you distinguish the difference between a spiritual awakening and a mental health challenge. They will help you move through this challenging time with supportive patience, to embrace the light and lessons when they are ready to be received.

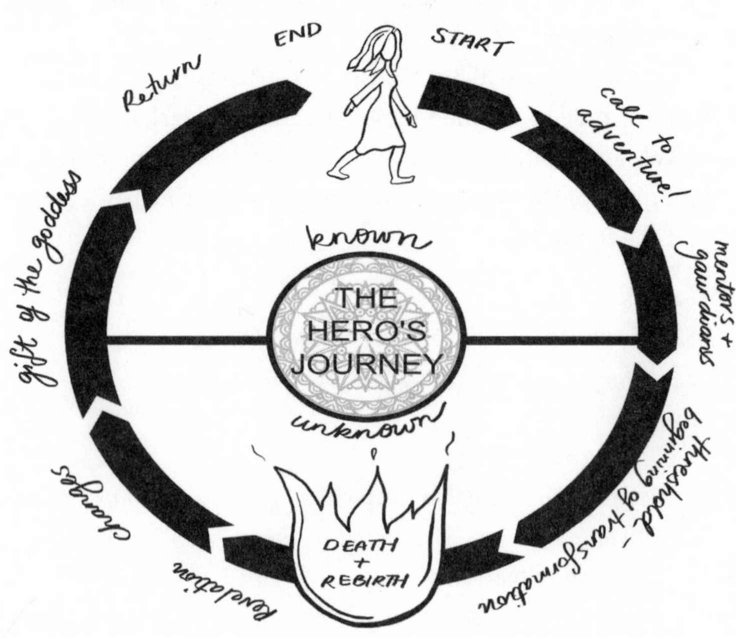

YOUR PHOENIX RISING

In ancient mythology, the phoenix is a unique bird that lived for five or six centuries in the Arabian Desert, after that time burning itself and rising from the ashes to start its next cycle.

Almost every culture has a version of the phoenix. With each rendition the themes are pretty consistent, with transformation, longevity and renewal being among the most potent meanings.

In the Western world, we most commonly celebrate the phoenix for its ability to die and come back to life, symbolising resurrection.

FAILURES, FLOPS, RESILIENCE AND BOUNCING BACK

Soulpreneurs are the kings and queens of the comeback, as occasional failures and flops are an inevitable part of taking risks and blazing your own path. Whether it be that you launch a product that no-one buys, release a book that no-one reads, an album that doesn't chart, or an event where only your friends buy tickets. It happens to the best of us.

Being able to cry in a ball on the floor, then dust ourselves off and step back up to another day of business takes supreme resilience. Soulpreneurship isn't for the faint-hearted. We are strong, we are determined. And this is why we need to stay tuned in to our why!

> *If Steve Jobs had quit, I wouldn't have all the devices that run my business nor written this book.*
> *If Oprah had quit, we wouldn't have SuperSoul Sessions.*

> *If Prince had quit, we wouldn't have the masterpiece that is Purple Rain.*
> *If Gal Gadot had quit, we wouldn't have her powerful portrayal of Wonder Woman!*

I'm going to share something personal with you here. A few years ago, I invested heavily in a client's event which failed so terribly that, for the first (and only) time, I needed to cancel the tour. I lost more money than I'd earned in my whole first year of business. Yet I still somehow dusted myself off and went on to create the two most successful tours of my career ... directly afterwards!

I went from the embarrassment and pain of my biggest financial failure to my then greatest successes in one leap. This isn't just luck. It's learning from the lessons. I've learnt far more from my failures than I have from my successes.

Failures have helped me become a stronger business coach, as I understand the agony, shame, disappointment and embarrassment attached to failing badly. Failures help me empathise and understand others in the same situation, which is all of us creatives or business owners at some stage!

Please don't give up. Always remember why you are doing this. Yes, there are times when we do need to pivot and course correct; just identify the difference between a bad day and a bad business.

Resilience is one of the most beautiful virtues that Soulpreneurs develop. Resilient people are able to integrate hard experiences into their lives in a way that makes them better. Embrace it, Soulpreneur! Failure is all part of the journey.

FACING CRITICISM

So you've started to quieten the inner critic. Now it's time to face the world, share your work and ... gulp! ... risk criticism.

Why do we care so much about what others think of us? Blog comments, book reviews, customer comment slips or end-of-event feedback forms—any form of criticism can be hard to stomach.

Our desperation to be liked is human nature anchored back into survival needs and staying part of the pack. It keeps us up at night and obsessively occupies our minds. Even if we've read 100 positive reviews or comments, we tend to laser focus in on that one niggly negative one! It clouds our thinking and sends us into a pit of despair: anger at those who criticise us, embarrassment about those who saw it, and the shame within ourselves of feeling like we are not good enough. It ignites and confirms our deepest darkest voice and thoughts.

If the criticism was public, it simulates the emotions and energy of a public hanging, a crucifixion. Dramatic? Yes. Genuine? Absolutely. In the darkest hours of the night, it's an unbearable and overblown feeling that loses all perspective. It hurts deeply.

Let's own that first—the raw and real emotions that criticism brings up. Because I know that, deep down, our feelings of being criticised, judged, rejected or disliked are what holds so many of us back from taking action on our dreams. So I'm not going to sugar-coat this ... criticism sucks!

And yet everyone who has ever done anything on a big scale has received criticism. Every one of my favourite musicians, authors, movies, books and blogs have received criticism. I'm so deeply grateful that those healers and creatives didn't give in to that, or let it stop them, because my life wouldn't be the same without them.

And my oh my! Have I been served up some criticism over the years, more than I used to think my sensitive soul could ever handle! Luckily it's only the tiniest fraction of all the comments that come my way, although I'm sure the volume will increase, as I continue to express and grow and reach more people. That's human nature.

And yes, it will continue to crush me, but I'm working on how I handle it. The more people we reach, the more risk we have of attracting and igniting new critics. It's part of the gig. Let's accept that. Let's make peace with that. Let's be discerning about the criticism we pay any attention to.

Musical legend Prince spoke of welcoming constructive criticism only from selected people. Author Brené Brown carries around a list in her wallet of the only people whose opinions she cares about. For me, there are peers I go to for guidance or feedback, as I value their views and they are 'in the ring' with me, putting themselves out there every day. They are not sitting anonymously behind keyboards or at the back of the stands, never doing anything themselves except criticising others.

The little boy who never followed his music dreams grows into the man who criticises successful musicians. The young girl who locked away her dreams of being a writer becomes the woman who leaves one-star reviews on Amazon, about books that she 'could have written better.' The teenagers who never fulfilled their sporting dreams hurl abuse at TV screens, when professional players aren't having their best game.

These are the critics we need to learn to ignore. As you'll see, that's most of them. Not all, but most of them.

Here are some suggestions to try when you're faced with critical feedback or a bad case of negativity:

- *Understand the difference between a 'troll' and a critic. Internet trolls wander around the internet day in day out stirring up trouble anywhere they can, whereas critics can occasionally have the positive intention of offering constructive feedback.*

- *Be honest and real with yourself. With a trusted friend or advisor, work through the criticism. Is there any truth in it? Is there something that can be improved? Is this comment coming from your target audience? Is this constructive feedback?*
- *Explore whether there has simply been a misunderstanding. Is an event attendee complaining about no food at an event, when it was clearly labelled a non-catered event? Did the book not cover something that it never promised to include?*
- *If it's a book or music reviewer, read their other reviews. Is it their usual style of review?*
- *If it's someone you know, determine what's going on in their business and life. Could you have triggered something that they are struggling with themselves?*
- *Respectfully ask for further explanation. A few years back, I was criticised about the cost of my services. I emailed back calmly, asking why they felt that way, whether I could help them or would they like info about our scholarships. I never even received a reply!*
- *Separate yourself from the criticism. When it's your soul work, this is hard to get into your head but your book is not you; your album is not you; your online course, intuitive reading or creative designs are not you. Please never validate your entire existence by the product or service you've created.*

Regardless of how nasty or negative the occasional critic may be, it's often the inner critic that lives in your head who is the nastiest. Making peace with your relationship with her first will make this a whole lot easier.

The more we love and accept our own work in the world, the less we seek the approval of others. While it's wonderful to receive glowing praise and testimonials, it can lock in a dependence on outside approval to feel proud.

This comes back down to our measurements of success in Chapter 2. Reflect back on how you feel fulfilled within yourself, without attaching to the approval of others or plugging in to their criticism. If your self-worth is measured by how high or low others think of you or your work, you are destined for a difficult life as a Soulpreneur!

I love the sign that my musician buddy and recording artist, Wes Carr, has up in his studio:

Set some goals.
Stay quiet about them.
Smash the shit out of them.
Clap for your own damn self.

Even with all the success in his life, including being crowned the winner of Australian Idol, Wes knows that we need to approve of our own art first. When others do too, it's simply a sweet bonus.

~ SOULPRENEUR SUCCESS SUMMARY ~

✓ *Decide on your comfort level with fame; be curious about your reasons for being seen and heard.*

✓ *Reflect on where you're at with your own stories.*

✓ *Consider privacy with other people's stories.*

✓ *Make sure you have the right support network and coping strategies in place, to deal with your darkness, failure, criticism and all that goes along with stepping into your spotlight.*

chapter ELEVEN

Expressing Your Creativity

Creativity is always a leap of faith.
You're faced with a blank page,
blank easel or an empty stage.
– **Julia Cameron**

Creativity isn't an elusive or exclusive gift just for artists and music makers; it's part of being a CEO, leader and solution-finder.

I believe we are all born with a capacity to be creative. We simply channel and express our creativity in different ways, which can be easy for some, harder for others.

Creativity allows us to problem-solve, to be innovative and to lead. Sometimes it flows, other times it doesn't. Regardless, don't fool yourself into thinking you are any less creative than others. This isn't an unreachable and rare magic. It's part of all of us.

Many of us grew up being encouraged to nurture and focus on facts and 'reality': logic, the analytical mind, accuracy, control, language, details, science and maths. Creativity is found more often in 'fantasyland': imagination, passion, art, music, intuition and risk-taking.

As Soulpreneurs, we need a balance of reality and fantasy, the details and the creativity. Over time, we may have buried our creativity deep down, hammering or squishing it, but it's still there. Our job isn't to unlock a box; it's to open the gates. To be free to fling those gates wide open, step through them and allow an unlimited abundant stream of creativity to flow through us onto the page, onto the stage, into our conversations, meetings, brainstorming and ideas.

There are guides walking beside you, trying to help you find the key to the gates, if only you will let them in and let them help you. As with everything, spiritual practice and improving your confidence will help, as it's confidence that tends to hold us back. Fears of criticism or rejection stop us in our tracks, blocking our stream of creativity.

Nothing will kill your creativity like your fear of failure or being laughed at. Comparisonitis jumps into play too. The fear that somebody else is creating something bigger or better than us is a real block. The fear you will never be as good as them, that people will laugh at you, ignore you, or compare you to everyone else doing everything 'better than you' ... these fears stem our creativity or dry it up completely.

You may feel that you aren't a 'creative person' because you don't know how to draw beyond stick figures, or you've never played an instrument, or you struggle to put an articulate sentence together, or you never seem to come up with breakthrough ideas in business meetings.

Yet even the most creative people I know—bestselling authors, chart-topping songwriters—compare their creativity to others. As young children we are so proud to show off our artwork. What happens? What changes? Why does creativity strike so much excitement and fear into our adult hearts?

Creativity is such a sensitive topic, as it is the expression of our soul and the innermost part of ourselves: our uncensored soul. We are sharing something that only we can see and hear, something so private. I've noticed three common challenges:

1. People who have forgotten how to be creative, even in the privacy of their own home.
2. People who are creative behind closed doors, but too scared to share with the world.
3. People who don't believe it's possible to 'make a living' from their creativity.

It gets easier with practice. Sharing a few words or sentences on social media is a great start. After that, move into blog posts, then into books, songs, podcasts and artwork.

> I was a different person before I started to write. When I realized I could be a songwriter and that people would listen—that was when I started feeling good in my life.
>
> – **Gwen Stefani**

UNLOCKING THE GATEWAY TO YOUR CREATIVITY

Our soul craves to create. Creativity is how our soul plays. At the same time, our soul needs to feel safe, welcome and invited to the creativity playground.

Surrounding yourself with inspiring people, books, movies, music and environments is a great place to start. That may be in the darkness of a movie cinema, watching a brilliant film. Other times it's in the car singing along to your favourite music; or walking in silence on the beach with your feet in the sand, the birds and waves the only sound in your ears. Even drinking a smoothie while chatting with an inspiring friend could do the trick!

My creativity and breakthroughs rarely come when sitting at my computer or being forced. Digital device overload is fuel for comparisonitis, not creativity.

Stop seeking your creative inspiration from others, especially those in your industry. Look outside your own backyard. Switch what you're reading or listening to. While writing business content, I only read spiritual texts. While writing spiritual content, I only read and watch fiction. Creating a pop album? Listen to folk music, or metal!

You never know where your inspiration is going to come from!

Everyone's creativity is unique. Everyone has a different routine or rhythm that ignites creativity. Some need to be well-rested and nourished, creating effortlessly in the morning after breakfast. Others stream creativity in the darkest hours of the night. Some thrive with a rigorous routine, putting in long hours. Others need to feel freedom and only create when inspired.

Is routine or spontaneity best for you? Explore all your options to see what works.

And move too! Google executives encourage their employees to play fun activities like volleyball and bowling, to activate the creative parts of their brains. This is great advice. Movement and keeping yourself busy with enjoyable activities will help keep your inner-creativity critic at bay, that voice telling you that your ideas aren't interesting, that everything has been said or done before, that no-one will enjoy what you are creating. That voice we all hear, yet all successful creatives choose to ignore.

Our inner-creativity critic is nastier and more negative than any review we will ever read about ourselves. Do you really want to spend the rest of your life listening to this false voice, who only exists in the shadows of your head? Or will you trust me and listen to your big, bright, beautiful soul who is begging you to open up the gateway to your creative confidence? Not to mention all the souls who are calling for your ideas, books, songs and creations.

We are all here ready and waiting for you to own and unlock the creativity that wants to pour through you. That patient stream has been building up behind the dam and is ready to burst through you. You have a lifetime of creativity waiting to go. It's time to unlock and open those floodgates!

One last note on creativity. You will never feel finished. I'm yet to finish creating a book, course, song, event or project that has ever felt finished. This is an ongoing dance I play with my inner perfectionist. Oh, she is such a drag! It exhausts me to even think about her! She always wants to point out how much better something could be, how many mistakes have been made, how much better everyone else's is, and how many bits or pieces need to be added for anything I ever do to be good enough.

Instead of bowing to her and her precious and perfect altar, I now turn the other way and roll my eyes.

> Every child is an artist; the problem is
> staying an artist when you grow up.
>
> – Pablo Picasso

RITUALS TO IGNITE CREATIVITY

> *Free-writing. Julia Cameron recommends Morning Pages in her classic book The Artist's Way. A couple of pages of longhand,*

stream-of-consciousness writing, done first thing in the morning. Uncensored, unedited.

- *Ride the waves. Some days it rains, some days in pours, other days it's a drought. There are days when I need to refill my creativity cup with a movie marathon or just do low-pressure admin work in my business.*
- *Stop trying (temporarily) and walk away. Go see a film or catch up with a friend instead. Then get back to it next day. Don't let this turn into week-long procrastination.*
- *Awaken your senses. Look at something beautiful, walk through an art gallery, smell fresh flowers, eat unusual foods, feel the ground beneath your bare feet, listen to music. I've shared my writing soundtracks at* **yvetteluciano.com/bookclub**.
- *Try creating at a different location or time of the day. While some creatives thrive with a daily routine, others require regular changes of schedule or environment.*
- *See a kinesiologist or healer, to ensure there are no fears or negative energies blocking you.*
- *Brainstorm with a friend, coach or Soulpreneur Buddy. Talking about your project or idea may get the creative juices flowing. Especially if you are a talker-thinker.*
- *Remove distractions; set up the right environment for you.*

GET MESSY

The number one way to ignite creativity and move through even the darkest writer's block is simply to write. Allow yourself to write, even if it's messy and not ever going to be used. Especially if it's messy!

Creating anything is a messy business. Know that you don't need to start at the beginning. It doesn't need to be linear. It doesn't need to make sense. The first chord or the first sentence is always the hardest. Just start. Write anything. Create any old how.

This is one time that I will say: *Push yourself!* No need to procrastinate or become paralysed with perfectionism. We need your music, your art, your words and your work.

As Brené Brown said: *Creativity is the way I share my soul with the world.*

Recently, I uncovered a common link between many of my creative friends. Most of us need to get down and dirty with our creativity. I'll put it nicely and say that I need to create in a beautiful mess. While I normally love a clean office, beautifully adorned desk, washed hair and morning exercise, that all goes out the window when I'm in a creative zone. The creative cocoon. The chrysalis.

As I type this chapter, I am surrounded by notebooks, crumpled up bits of paper with illegible scribble, sage ashes, spilled candle wax, stacks of oracle cards flung out of their boxes, essential oil bottles that have misplaced lids, toast crusts and stained cups with day-old teabags, dirty cutlery and a random roll of paper towels, which I recall was for cleaning up a spilled smoothie several days ago.

It's amusing that my morning writing ritual is lighting a candle for the soul of the book, and anointing myself with beautiful oils for her, yet I can't even manage putting a bra on for visitors right now. The doors are bolted shut. Yep, this is the grotty, messy middle. Honestly, it's all a little feral. I don't remember the last time I washed my hair. I don't think I even unpacked my hairbrush from the suitcase, when I returned from a trip almost a week ago. Oh dear god! Have I even opened the suitcase since returning?

I'm sure you are getting the picture. For me, this is how I create best. When I do take a glance around my office, or catch sight of the abandoned shampoo in my shower, at least I know it isn't this messy always. Heavens no! In two weeks, I'll be back to my clean, pulled together self once again. Out in the world with my organised, extrovert, clean face on. Then it will be my husband's turn to enter his creative cave, and I'll be the one reminding him to shower and drink his smoothies.

If you are someone who can maintain a clean, structured and organised life while in the creative process, I bow to you! We are all different and need to find ways that work for us. We don't all have the luxury of cocooning ourselves away from the world for a week, yet do try to find moments when you can. During a lunch break, late on a Friday night, or first thing in the morning before the world wakes up.

There are times when I just need to grab creative moments here and there. Find the time and ways to make it work. And remember, when you do find those micro-moments, start by asking the soul of your work one simple question: *What would you like to co-create together today?*

~ SOULPRENEUR SUCCESS SUMMARY ~

✓ *Reflect on the different ways you solve problems creatively.*

✓ *Try different types, places and times for getting creative; see what works for you.*

✓ *Experiment with different styles of creativity.*

✓ *Allow yourself to get messy when creating.*

part THREE

Platform

chapter TWELVE

Leading with Love and Light

We teach best what we most need to learn.

– **Richard Bach**

TRANSFORMATION FROM STUDENT TO TEACHER

Stepping up and out as a leader or a teacher can stir up those old self-worth issues. Especially if we are speaking, writing or teaching from personal experiences. And yet, the best wellness teachers come from illness. The best sobriety teachers come from addiction. The most powerful self-acceptance teachers come from breakdown, from bullying, from eating disorders, from body shame.

You don't need be fully healed or have a spotless background to be a teacher or leader; you just need to be a few steps ahead of where your students are. Own your shadow, own your scars, own your transformational stories that taught you the greatest lessons. Own your experiences as a student of life that have transformed you into the teacher you were born to be.

While I was terrible at school and that study environment, I've thrived in on-the-spot or on-the-job learning. And I'm a very thorough student of life. All of my favourite teachers are. While I may have been a C-grade average school student, I believe I'm an A-grade student in the school of life.

You don't need to be perfect; you just need to be prepared to share openly. This may mean coming out of the 'spiritual closet,' if you're publishing personal stories, which is why self-care and sharing with discernment is so important.

Be honest about where you are, what you know, what you don't and what you can share, so others can learn from you. Take them on the journey with you, because we are all in this together.

ACTIVISM

> Activism is the rent I pay for
> living on the planet.
>
> – Alice Walker

Soulpreneurship for you may mean making genuine change in the world. Which isn't all rainbows and unicorns. As lightworkers, we must be brave to dive into the dark at times.

The new age and personal development world has been known to encourage us to share 'positive vibes only,' and turn away from the news, world issues or confronting conversations. There are times when I believe this is helpful. I understand the need to protect your fragile heart, especially if you are facing a serious health diagnosis or the death of a loved one.

However for the rest of the time, we must pull up our big girl pants and face the fact that if we won't stand up, speak up and make a difference, who will? Why must political, environmental or human rights issues be dealt with by other people, not us?

Our sensitive and empathetic souls can be put to good use here. Because we care so deeply, because we are so compassionate. Because we aren't afraid to lose social media followers or an unaligned customer base. Because we are here to do work that is much bigger than just us.

Gala Darling wrote that: *You are not insane if you're feeling afraid, anxious, nauseous or mad as hell when watching the news. No, you're not insane at all. In fact, if you're feeling that way, you know what? Your moral compass is intact. This is the only human way to feel.*

For Soulpreneurs, it's far better to put this feeling—this rage—to good use, rather than let it fester inside us or simply fill up our Facebook feeds. Your rage has a purpose. That rage, those tears, your anxiety on hearing about mistreatment of animals, the planet or our people is here to activate you. It's here to ignite a calling. It chose you.

Ignorance is not bliss. Like all pain in our lives, the more we try to deny or supress it, the more it will turn ugly.

Fortunately, the best way to heal this part of us is to take action in the highest good for everyone. In your moment of fury, take a few deep breaths, meditate, pray to your guides and ask them to show you the way, to guide you towards the actions you **can** take.

Need some suggestions?

> *Use your platform for good.*
> *Sign, share or create petitions for local government.*
> *Learn about the political candidates and parties in your state and country.*
> *Attend or organise peaceful protests and rallies.*

- *Educate others and empower them to make a difference too.*
- *Throughout all of your business and marketing, ensure that your posts, imagery and products do not segregate or discriminate on the basis of race, gender, ability or religion.*
- *Donate a percentage of your profits to charities and causes you care about.*
- *Organise fundraisers.*
- *Get a group of Soulpreneurs together for a shared cause.*
- *Speak with your wallet, by ensuring your purchases are not funding unethical treatment of animals, people or the planet.*

Stand up and speak up. Lead by example. What you say or speak in your homes, in front of your children, in the post office queue or in the doctor's waiting room influences your family and your community. As does not speaking up, when you hear hateful or harmful words being spoken.

> I will fight—for those who cannot fight for themselves.
>
> – Wonder Woman

PATIENCE AND PERSISTENCE

> Patience, persistence and perspiration make an unbeatable combination for success.
>
> – Napoleon Hill

Creating a business or building a platform is never easy and rarely fast. Fun? It can be! Exciting? Yes! Fulfilling? Absolutely! Easy though? Not always.

True success, soulful success, tends to be built at a slow and steady pace, requiring patience, persistence and perspiration together with an inwardly positive and outwardly helpful attitude.

Preparing and making peace with the pace of the process is ideal. While I encourage you to take some of the shortcuts that present themselves, remember to always check in on their alignment with the soul of your business.

Don't let the bright shiny lights take your eye off the prize. Stay focused on your vision, keeping the reason why you started and who you are here to serve front and centre. Making a true difference doesn't happen overnight.

Go with grace, go with ease. It doesn't always need to be a long and hard road. Just accept that sometimes it won't be without obstacles.

Embrace taking your time to build an organic audience, instead of buying followers. Create genuine relationships, rather than buy your way into opportunities. It will pay off in the long run.

Take your time. Do it right the first time. Be patient. Focus on the long game. Don't compare yourself to everyone else's pace. Stay in your own lane and remember this isn't a race.

~ SOULPRENEUR SUCCESS SUMMARY ~

✓ *Define what your platform is here to do: teach, activate, organise and share.*

✓ *Build your platform gradually and patiently.*

chapter THIRTEEN

Income, Offerings and Operations

> Great things are not done by impulse, but a series of small things brought together.
>
> – Vincent Van Gogh

SETTING UP YOUR BUSINESS WITH BRICKS, NOT STICKS

While you have big visions and it certainly feels more fun and colourful to create brand logos and set up social media channels, all successful Soulpreneur businesses need to lay a solid foundation.

In this chapter, we dive into the first chakra of your business, the base chakra. The legal and financial foundations upon which your business will be secure and thrive. While knowing your audience, dreams, vision and mission will drive you, and having an abundant mindset is super helpful, let's now get clarity on **how** the money is coming in the door.

It's clarity time! How will you make money? What are your products and services that will feed you and pay to fuel your mission and dreams?

SOULPRENEUR STEPS

List all potential revenue streams that you're considering, e.g. digital products, physical products, coaching, consulting, talks or performances:

....

....

....

....

Pick one or two specific products or services that you can start working on immediately. Preferably start creating your offers one at a time. The simpler the better. Remember there needs to be ease and joy in creating these. What feels good for you and uses your natural gifts and talents?

Tap into the empathy you have with your audience. What will help solve their problems, ease their pain, or inspire them to be happier or healthier? Research your audience. What do they need?

If you are still unsure, you may need to laser in on an industry you are passionate about, such as health, fitness, yoga, food, art or music. Then take a look at the multiple models you can explore.

For example, if you love yoga, there are more options than just teaching local in-person classes. Other opportunities include:

hosting online programs, creating or writing for yoga magazines, writing books, filming documentaries, hosting workshops or teacher training, designing cool yoga tights or even producing music for yoga classes! Maybe you can help other yoga teachers build their businesses and nurture their communities, using admin or marketing skills from previous roles.

If you need more help, go back to Chapter 1 where we explored your 'talents' in the Truth Trifecta and Chapter 6 where we visualised your audience's desires. Think about how these tie in with your current and desired lifestyle.

For example, if you're a new mother, a one-on-one coaching schedule may not work for you. Instead, perhaps you need something super flexible that allows you to work spontaneously in between baby naps. Content creation in your own time might be a more ideal alternative right now. On the other hand, if you're an extrovert with an open schedule, you may thrive with a full schedule of clients booked in for face-to-face work.

Keep all this in mind when selecting what products and services you will sell and create.

BUSINESS START-UP 101

While I cannot give you specific financial or legal advice, I can give you the questions to start asking yourself and help you navigate your way to the people you need.

Here is a basic **business plan template**. Use this as a simple guide when preparing your own business plan.

Business Plan Template

Business Name: ______________________________.

Summary: [your business name] is a ____________________ that provides ________________ for ____________________ to help them ____________________.

(You can also weave in why and when business was started.)

Objectives and Intentions: Vision, mission, sales numbers, customer numbers next year and in the future. For example:

Attract ________________ clients by ________________

Receive ________ in income by ____________ or ________ every month

Increase clients or income by ________________

Action Plan Overview, Timeline and Resources to Achieve Objectives:

To complete ________________ [action] by ________________ [date] will require ________________ [resources]

Resources: Premises, equipment, software, staff.

Target Audience: Age, gender, marital status, beliefs, values, consumption patterns, income, location, likes, dislikes, highs, lows, challenges etc.

Market Analysis: Who else do they love in your industry, what makes you different, your twist, your wow, your uniqueness, what they need that isn't yet available or accessible to them?

Products and Services: List 3-5 products and services including price.

Marketing and Promo: PR, website, digital platforms, media coverage, advertising, speaking, writing, blogging, connecting (networking), collaborating.

Team: Key members, org chart, advisors, size, operations.

Finance: $________ is required for start-up costs:

Item	Cost	Required
Logo and website design and development	$5000	As above timeline
Computer, phone etc.		

Options to source start-up costs: Loan, savings, crowdfunding etc.

Projected Income: How long until you break even and start making a profit?

Business check-up

Once you have established your business plan, check in on the business basics at regular intervals. You can also add details in this exercise, which you can return to again and again as you build or grow your business in the future. Please do not be daunted by the detail, as many elements may not yet apply to you. This is based on start-ups in Australia.

SOULPRENEUR STEPS

Answer these questions to put in place a more **detailed support system** for your business.

Structure

Are you a sole trader, partnership (names of partners), company (names of directors/co sec, shareholders) or trust (type of trust and name of trustee)?

....

Advisors and specialists

What advisors or specialists do you have or need? (Tick box and add name where appropriate.)

☐ Coach ____________________.

☐ Accountant and/or bookkeeper ____________________.

☐ Legal (trademarks etc.) ____________________.

☐ Marketing ____________________.

☐ Market research ____________________.

☐ IT: systems, domain, website ____________________.

☐ Graphic designer ____________________.

☐ Production/operations ____________________.

☐ HR ____________________.

☐ Import/export ____________________.

☐ Insurance ____________________.

☐ Finance broker ____________________.

☐ Business broker ____________________.

☐ Freight/shipping broker ____________________.

Planning

What do you need to have in place? (Tick box and add response where appropriate.)

☐ Business plan ____________________.

☐ Marketing plan ____________________.

☐ Export plan ____________________.

☐ Projects ____________________.

☐ Research ____________________.

☐ Succession plan ____________________.

☐ Emergency and recovery plan ____________________.

Finance

How much money will you need to get started?

Where will these funds come from? (Tick box and add response where appropriate.)

☐ Self: savings/mortgage ____________________.

☐ Family ____________________.

☐ Friends ____________________.

☐ Bank: loan/credit card/overdraft ____________________.

☐ Investors ____________________.

☐ Shareholders ____________________.

☐ Government: grants/subsidies ____________________.

☐ Barter ____________________.

☐ Vendor ____________________.

☐ Franchisor ____________________.

☐ Crowdfunding ____________________.

Regulatory and compliance

Which of these do you need to research or action? (Tick box and add response where appropriate.)

☐ Business name ____________________.

☐ ACN/ABN ____________________.

☐ Trademark/patent/copyright ____________________.

☐ State: stamp duty/land tax/payroll tax ____________________.

☐ Local: rates/licences/permits ____________________.

☐ ACCC: consumer law/product safety standards ____________________.

☐ Privacy ____________________.

☐ TGA ____________________.

☐ Industry codes of practice/regulation ____________________.

☐ Industry association membership ____________________.

☐ Franchising code of conduct ____________________.

☐ Customs ____________________.

☐ ATO: TFN/GST/excise/PAYG/FBT/PSI ____________________.

Staff

Which of these do you need to research or action? (Tick box and add response where appropriate.)

☐ Organisational ____________________.

☐ Culture ____________________.

☐ Delegation ____________________.

☐ Recruitment ____________________.

☐ Apprentices/trainees/interns ____________________.

☐ Award/Fair Work Australia ____________________.

☐ Contractors ____________________.

☐ Equal opportunity/anti-discrimination ____________________.

☐ Work health and safety/Australian WH&S ____________________.

☐ Superannuation ____________________.

☐ Training ____________________.

☐ WorkCover ____________________.

Premises and set-up

Which of these do you need? (Tick box and add response where appropriate.)

☐ Website ____________________.

☐ Home or office ____________________.

- ☐ Purchase or lease ___________________.
- ☐ ISP ___________________.
- ☐ Telecoms ___________________.
- ☐ Furniture ___________________.
- ☐ Equipment ___________________.
- ☐ Computers ___________________.
- ☐ Motor vehicles ___________________.
- ☐ Parking/transport ___________________.
- ☐ Customer access/convenience ___________________.

OTHER SOULPRENEUR SET-UPS

As an alternative or addition to your own products and services, other popular income streams for Soulpreneurs are through affiliate programs, sponsorships or network marketing. These are becoming increasingly popular for good reason and I selectively embrace all of these as part of my business nowadays.

Why do I say 'selectively'? It's important to be discerning and aligned in what you choose to invest your time into and share with your loved and loyal audience, only collaborating with people and companies that you have researched thoroughly, know intimately and use personally.

For example, I'm a proud affiliate partner with Gabrielle Bernstein and have a network marketing partnership with dōTERRA essential oils. Soulful partnerships and generous income streams enable me to be more flexible and generous with my other products, services and offerings.

I could comfortably thrive on these abundant financial foundations alone, which means that all the other work I do in the world, including writing this book and all the free resources at **yvetteluciano.com/bookclub**, come from a pure place of service, and not a need to pay my bills!

The new wave of affiliate and network marketing is upon us. Try to have an open mind and heart, and explore the opportunities that may be calling to your soul.

Business gurus Tony Robbins and Gary Vaynerchuk sing the praises of network marketing. Robert Kiyosaki, investor and author of the classic *Rich Dad, Poor Dad,* has said: *If I had to do it all over again, rather than build an old-style type of business, I would have started building a network marketing business. Network marketing gives people the opportunity, with very low risk and very low financial commitment, to build their own income-generating asset and acquire great wealth.*

And I have to say I agree, although what I love most is the collaboration and camaraderie. When I look back on those years of doing everything all on my own from scratch, I can see how network marketing would have served and supported me along that journey.

These business options are all evolving. The future is now. And it's exciting!

PARTNERSHIPS, MENTORS, MASTERMINDS AND COLLABORATIONS

> As you navigate through the rest of your life, be open to collaboration. Find a group of people who challenge and inspire you, spend a lot of time with them, and it will change your life.
>
> – **Amy Poehler**

There is no way I could have created my businesses and success on my own. It's only been possible thanks to mentors, masterminds and collaborations. I've found that being part of supportive mastermind groups with intimate groups of entrepreneurial friends to be priceless. These women are at similar stages of business to me, with the same desire to follow their soul's path.

The great news is that you can start your own! Put it out to the Universe. Go out to the other souls around you who are at the same stage as you in business. Come together and support each other.

You could create an online group, regular group video calls or working retreats together. Alternatively, you can invest in a paid mastermind where the leader creates the group, holds the space and coaches the members. Masterminds help 'solopreneurs' feel a sense of camaraderie and team. They're also where many of my deepest friendships have been formed.

Additionally or instead, you can work with a **mentor** one-on-one. This could be a dedicated business coach who you pay to have regular sessions, or someone who is a couple of steps ahead of you in your industry and happy to help you from their experiences.

A great mentor match is one who:

- *inspires you with their integrity, credibility and track record*
- *you respect and admire*
- *encourages you to step outside your comfort zone and lovingly challenges you*
- *understands your industry and your audience*

Another one of my favourite ways of working is in **partnerships and collaborations**; however, it can also be the most challenging. Some pointers to bear in mind:

- *All collaborations must be built on a solid foundation of mutual trust and respect.*
- *Ensure values are aligned. Know each other's Truth Trifectas and honour them.*
- *Be on the same page with the future vision and intentions.*
- *An equal investment of energy, time or money needs to be felt between all involved.*

HIRING TEAM MEMBERS

It's exciting when your business is growing and there is some income to invest in hiring official team members to support continued growth. While I don't want to burst any bubbles for you, I will be honest here. Finding and keeping aligned team members can be one of the greatest challenges for Soulpreneurs.

And that is something I didn't want to hear—in fact, totally ignored!—when I was beginning. I had the vision of a big group of gal pals all having a blast working together. Was that a hangover from The Baby-Sitters Club books?

Please don't get me wrong; many of the team members I've hired over the years have become great lifelong friends. However, many ... well ... haven't. It's thanks to my mastermind groups with incredible leaders that I know how common this challenge can be for other Soulpreneurs. I know it all too well.

Here are some suggestions from the lessons I've learnt and those of other leading Soulpreneurs:

> *Try freelancers and contractors first. This will help you get clear on what you need, and what type of personalities and skills will suit you and your business.*
> *When hiring, write clear job descriptions. Focus on the benefits and the challenges of the role.*
> *Check out social media profiles.*
> *Do thorough reference checks. Ensure the reference you are calling was actually the up-line or manager of the applicant, not just a colleague.*
> *Understand the intentions of the applicant. Ask them to do the Truth Trifecta exercise.*
> *Passion and enthusiasm trumps the skills and tasks that can be learnt.*
> *Ensure they have a deep understanding and love of your audience.*
> *Have a probationary or trial period.*
> *Pay attention to how they talk about their previous employers and colleagues.*

Start-up businesses can have many highs and lows. Your team will need to be positive, optimistic and resilient as they ride the waves. Attitude is everything.

If deep down someone isn't the right fit or you don't trust them, let them go as early as possible.

If they are a good fit with the right attitude and you trust them, take the time to train them and nurture them. Involve them in your decision-making processes, ensuring they feel like part of the team. They will become one of your business' greatest gifts.

OPERATING A GREEN ECO-FRIENDLY BUSINESS

The last area I want to cover when it comes to the practicalities of operating your business is going green. If setting up from scratch, you have an opportunity to implement eco-friendly practices from the start. If you're already in business and you're looking at soul-aligned ops, these ideas are great to explore.

Go paperless! Avoid having a printer at home. I did this for the first years of my business. Anything important was emailed to the local printers. Knowing I had to walk a long way to get my printing done meant I never printed anything that wasn't 100% necessary.

Plastic bottle ban: I banned plastic bottles from every single Earth Events stage.

Recycle and reuse: Especially all that packaging! Buy refurbished digital devices and recycled furniture.

Save electricity: Turn computers, chargers and lights off when not in use.

Choosing suppliers: Do your research and prioritise green vendors.

Save petrol: If appropriate, do more phone or skype meetings, save up errands and do them all in one trip, and think carefully about travel choices. Carbon offset flights and events.

~ SOULPRENEUR SUCCESS SUMMARY ~

✓ *Write your business plan.*

✓ *Identify your support systems, professionals and reporting.*

✓ *Discern additional income streams, such as affiliate partnerships and network marketing.*

✓ *Start building an aligned team.*

✓ *See where you could introduce more soulful eco-friendly business policies.*

chapter FOURTEEN

Your Beautiful Brand

Your brand is what other people say about you when you're not in the room.

– **Jeff Bezos**

BRANDING THAT ALIGNS WITH YOU

Your brand is much bigger than your logo or business cards. It's how your audience recognise and resonate with the soul of your business.

Your brand encompasses the senses. It influences how your audience sees, hears and feels when experiencing your work. Your brand is the outfit, the earth suit for the soul of your business, when it's out there sharing your work and message. You want to take loving care of your brand, to help it be attractive, vibrant, clear and magnetic to your audience and all the souls who need your work.

It's said that we have as little as five seconds to make a first impression, and this can rarely be changed. So you need to put your best foot forward, right from the beginning.

In this chapter, we'll start from scratch to either build your beautiful brand from the ground up, or check in and refresh your existing branding.

While some companies spend all their branding efforts and budget on fancy logos or artwork, which are important, it's important to recognise that this is only **part** of branding for Soulpreneurs. What you will discover in this chapter is that a successful brand is positive, consistent, accessible and inspirational. Whether potential fans are purchasing a product from you, scrolling through your social media posts or attending your event, they are experiencing your brand. It's your opportunity to improve their day and build a loyal fan for life.

NON-NEGOTIABLES OF BRAND SUCCESS

These are the six non-negotiables for your brand's success. Each one is followed by some questions for you to consider about your brand.

Trust

When your audience trusts you, they will not only stay with you and feel comfortable buying from you, but will also feel confident recommending you to others.

Trust cannot be bought, and must be earned. Your audience will trust your actions, more than your words. Lead by example. Trust can take weeks or months to build, and over the years it will continue to grow. Do remember that trust can be damaged in an instant, and is a make or break factor for many brands.

> *What will help your audience feel safe buying from you?*
> *Do they know enough about your brand?*

- *Do people trust the story of your brand and the people behind it?*
- *Does the brand have integrity?*
- *Have your audience or people they know had positive experiences with the brand?*

Uniqueness

While you don't need to be entirely unique and original to create a successful brand, it is worthwhile exploring what your 'twist' or slightly unique take is among your peers.

Your uniqueness may be features, functions or pricing, although the most powerful way to differentiate from others in the market is through your story, where you can have an emotional connection.

- *How is your brand different from others in your market?*
- *Does your audience feel your brand is different enough from what they already have?*
- *Is there a topic where you want to be the 'go to' expert?*
- *What is the 'twist' in your story or brand?*

Authenticity

Authenticity is the best way to develop trust and be different or unique in the market. While it's a big word thrown around online, let's get back to the core of what authenticity really is: transparency and alignment. It's matching what we say and do on the outside, with who we are and what we believe on the inside. It's letting go of who we think we should be, and embracing who we truly are.

Those who are truly authentic will be ahead of the competition as it's impossible for anyone to be exactly like us when we are all in true authenticity. This will not only improve your brand and business, but all parts of your life. This is about keeping it real.

> *How are you sharing authentically with your audience?*
> *Are there things that you could do or share differently that are in more alignment?*

Consistency

Being consistent helps your audience feel they can depend on you. They feel safe and comfortable in the direction you are steering them.

Consistency is maintaining the quality of your products and services, and the quantity that you are delivering. This includes the frequency of your social media posts and consistent positioning on particular topics and messages, rather than the occasional actions you take.

Consistency is continuing to show up in a way that your audience recognises, resonates with and trusts!

> *How can you increase brand consistency across all platforms and experiences?*

Memorability

Your name and the look of your brand needs to be memorable, and this is heightened through a memorable experience with the business, such as a story or moment that your audience can't forget. This might be an online interaction or in person event.

Give your audience a memorable moment for the right reasons and they are guaranteed to return and recommend you to others. Word of mouth or referral is the most valuable form of marketing around.

> *Is your brand easy to remember, to return to, and to recommend to others?*

Community

Your audience needs to identify with your brand and associate themselves with you loud and proud. This goes back to ancient times, as human beings we love to fit in and connect. In our modern lives, brands help us do just that.

Look to the health world and you'll see many examples of communities: paleos, vegans, crossfitters, spirit junkies. See how they connect a group of people who share a belief? And by wearing a clothing or jewellery brand, we tell the world a lot about our beliefs and values, showing which community are part of.

> *Would your audience feel proud to be seen as part of your community and make you part of their life?*

SOULPRENEUR STEPS

Now think of some brands you love. **Describe why you love them**, by reflecting on the six brand non-negotiables.

Why do you trust them?

....

....

How are they unique from others in the market?

....

....

How do they convey their authenticity?

....

....

Are their posts, products, services and experiences consistent?

....

....

Are you proud to be part of their community?

....

....

Are they easy to remember and recommend to others?

....

....

PERSONAL VERSUS COMPANY BRAND

The next aspect you need to establish is whether you're a personal brand or company brand. Deciding which you want to be will save you a lot of rebranding down the track and is simply about being clear on your priorities. Let's look at the difference.

A **personal brand** is built around your name and image. Reasons to choose a personal brand:

> *Establishing a speaking or writing career*
> *Being your industry standard (artists, singers, coaches, teachers)*
> *Being easier for your audience to connect with you*

A **company brand** is created from scratch and sets the tone for your business. You may prefer to start a company brand, if you wish to eventually sell your business or bring in partners.

Some examples of personal and company brands:

> *Author and speaker Deepak Chopra has a personal brand.*
> *Publishing company Hay House is an example of a company brand.*
> *TV host and producer Oprah Winfrey is a personal brand.*
> *Her TV network OWN and publishing company O Magazine are company brands.*

If you've already invested time and money into one or the other, you don't need to ditch it altogether if you decide to change. Brand names can become taglines, book titles or project names.

So now it's decision time! What will you name your business?

If you're a personal brand, this question is reasonably easy. Your business name is simply your own name! Of course, if your name is common or already in use by someone well known, you may wish to use a nickname, middle name, initials, maiden name or even a stage name. There are ways to make it work.

If you're choosing a company name, consider the following:

- Create a name completely from scratch like *Google*.
- Come up with a descriptive name like *The Body Shop*.

- Use alliteration like *Earth Events.*
- Or a rhyme like *YouTube.*

Ensure the tone of the name matches the emotion! If you want your audience to feel warm and fuzzy, then acronyms (*BMW*) and tech-sounding names (*Xerox*) aren't for you.

Set the tone and values, like Jessica Alba's *The Honest Company.*

Even if you have a personal brand, you can use this exercise to develop project or product sub-brands, like Sarah Wilson's *I Quit Sugar* or Belinda Davidson's *School of the Modern Mystic.*

VISUAL IDENTITY

This is how your audience will see you. It is arguably one of the most important brand elements and one worth investing in from the beginning, to save lots of time, energy and expense down the track.

Logo

Your logo is the graphic identity, emblem, icon, representation or symbol of your company name or trademark. Try not to obsess about this and remember that many of the most respected and recognised logos are simple and easy to recognise. It will appear on your products, website, in your email signature, stationary and anywhere else you wish to stamp with your professional identity.

Start collecting references and examples of logos, and describe what you like and why. This will help your graphic designer understand the type of logo you would like.

Colours

Even the most simple colour palette of a couple of primary colours and a few secondary colours will do wonders!

Pick colours that resonate with you and your audience, using the guide below:

Purple
Spirituality
Fantasy
Royalty
Wisdom
Wealth
Imagination

Yellow
Self esteem
Cheerfulness
Warmth
Energy
Attention
Optimism

Blue
Water
Peace
Serenity
Trust
Communication
Truth
Dependable
Masculine

Orange
Confidence
Excitement
Enthusiasm
Friendly
Impulsive
Pleasure
Creativity
Motivation

Green
Nature
Health
Growth
Environment
Tranquillity
Fertility
Wealth and money

Red
Strong
Appetite
Passion
Intensity
Love
Bold
Urgency

Fonts
With the help of a trusted designer, either select a consistently available font or custom-create one.

COMMUNICATIONS

Yes, the way you speak, write and listen are all part of the branding mix. While visuals convey a feeling, your communications often directly tell people what's what. Of course, this shows a lot about who you are, what your Soulpreneur business stands for, and the kind of connection your audience can expect.

Personality and emotion

When you communicate with your audience, consider how you want to come across and how you want them to feel. Go back to your Truth Trifecta and pull out any personality traits for your brand. Look for words like:

> *ambitious, brave, bright, calm, cool, creative, down-to-earth, entertaining, friendly, funny, generous, gentle, healthy, helpful, honest, innovative, kind, knowledgeable, luxurious, mature, peaceful, powerful, relatable, revolutionary, spiritual, stylish, upbeat, warm, wise, young*

These need to align with your audience, to ensure you are attracting and keeping the right customers and clients. How does your audience feel when they see or experience your brand? How do you want them to feel? What emotions do you wish to trigger in your audience?

Consider the following pairs of words which are opposed in meaning. Which words relate to how your audience perceives your brand?

- *high-end/affordable*
- *premium/value*
- *high-quality/accessible*
- *innovative/established*
- *risky/reliable*
- *formal/friendly*
- *exclusive/mainstream*
- *wholesome/naughty*

- *sweet/sassy*
- *polished/raw*
- *modern/ancient*
- *new/traditional*
- *treat/everyday*

Language and voice

Consider the key words, language and voice of your brand. What is the general tone and attitude? Is there a way that you do or do not wish to communicate with your audience? What is your brand's vocabulary? Are there words to always include and words to avoid?

For example, communications from Disney frequently include *magic, kingdom, fantasy, dreams* and consistently omit negative or curse words.

Slogans and taglines

It's also handy to have sound bites, catchphrases and one-liners that instantly identify your brand. The intention is to capture attention, be easy to understand and memorable.

For example:

- *Just Do It*
- *Think different*
- *Because you're worth it*
- *There are some things money can't buy. For everything else, there's …*

In the early stages of your business, your taglines will probably evolve. My PR company, Earth HQ, began with 'creating positive change' and evolved into 'creating a happier, healthier world.' Next we moved to 'having fun, healing the world together.'

Start playing with emotive keywords now. The trick, as always, is to keep it simple.

Story and beliefs

According to Simon Sinek: *People don't buy what you do; they buy why you do it.* This implies that your audience connects via a common belief, background or story.

In Chapter 10, we talked about being in the spotlight and sharing personal stories, as a way of connecting with your audience. Remember your business itself has a soul too, and a story. Reflect on the journey your business has been through and the values it represents.

> *What is your brand's story?*
> *What are the beliefs of the brand?*
> *What do you want your audience to share about your brand?*

Your beliefs need to be identical to the beliefs of your audience. Your story needs to be repeatable by your loyal followers. And your mission needs to be inspirational to them.

SOULPRENEUR STEPS

If you had twenty to thirty seconds in front of your dream client, publisher, event promotor or TV producer, how would you describe who you are, what you do, why you do it and how you can help them?

We've all heard of the 'elevator pitch' that entrepreneurs are asked to create, to sell in an idea or product to potential investors. Let's call ours an 'elevate speech.'

The idea of an elevate speech isn't to pitch or sell in anything. Instead it's to engage with the person we are speaking with and elevate their energy through the conversation, which in turn uplifts and opens up to a discussion about your products and services. So that, even if you do only get thirty seconds with someone, they are open to give you their email address or phone number so you can continue the conversation.

Draft your **elevate speech**, so you leave a memorable impression when you have opportunities to connect:

....

....

....

....

....

....

....

AUDIENCE AND MESSAGE

Once you've dived deep into creating and establishing your brand, think about how your audience will find you.

There are so many ways for you to market and promote yourself these days, so your audience might find you almost anywhere. Examples include a blog, podcast, digital magazine, speaking at events, free ebooks and videos (either as a guest or making them yourself).

SOULPRENEUR STEPS

List all potential **marketing and promotional streams** that your audience would enjoy.

....

....

....

....

Check the following, if you already have a brand:

> *Look over all your digital platforms*
> *Consider your photos*
> *Check your email newsletters and email signatures*
> *Google yourself*
> *Ask your existing audience and customers*

YOUR SOUL'S STYLE

The last part is making it all happen. It's time to call in the professionals to help bring your brand to life.

Your brand squad may include a photographer, stylist, designer, web developer and copywriter. Finding the right team to balance style with soul may take a while, but it's worth it in the end.

Here's what to do:

> *Get clear on your budget and invest as much as you can afford.*
> *Source all the price quotes you need, then Skype or call them to get an idea of their vibe. It's ideal if they are your target market too.*

- > *Check your contractors' portfolios and speak with previous clients if you can.*
- > *Ensure expectations are aligned on deadlines and delivery times.*
- > *Collate style references and examples of what you love.*
- > *Reference other brands and designs, but make sure yours are different and do not infringe on IP or trademarks. Imitation is not the highest form of flattery—it's just immoral, hurtful and can be illegal.*
- > *Ensure you receive a style guide. Everyone in your team (now and in the future) needs it.*

You deserve branding that you are proud of and is magnetic to your audience. Keep it simple and remember that branding is an ongoing, long-term project. Refresh occasionally or overhaul completely, but know you don't need to have perfect branding to begin working with your audience. Just get started and have fun with it!

~ SOULPRENEUR SUCCESS SUMMARY ~

✓ *Define your brand through the six brand non-negotiables.*

✓ *Reflect on what you love about the brands you admire.*

✓ *Decide on the visual and communications style of your brand.*

✓ *Craft your brand story and personality.*

✓ *Hire experts to help you put out a professional brand.*

✓ *Decide where you will promote.*

chapter FIFTEEN

Embracing the Digital World

The internet is becoming the town square
for the global village of tomorrow.

– **Bill Gates**

When people are faced with challenges these days, they turn to the web. Whether they're having a bad day, facing a health crisis, considering a new career direction, experiencing heartbreak, searching for life purpose or wondering how to make a smoothie.

And you, beautiful Soulpreneur, can be right there, ready to serve them, soothe them and solve their problems with your own mini media empire. Today is one of the greatest and most fortunate times to be rising up and sharing your work with the world, because we can embrace the digital world **on our terms**.

MEDIA STRATEGY CONSIDERATIONS

Before diving into digital platforms specifically, let's take a moment to talk about the different types of media available to us as Soulpreneurs, to illustrate why going digital is so special for us sovereign souls. In effect, there are two paths we could go down as we create our digital platforms. Either try to gain attention out there in the world or attract it towards us like a magnet.

To understand the distinction, let's use an analogy we all understand. I'm sure you've heard the theory that the singles who are always on the hunt for someone to 'complete them' tend to repel prospective partners, whereas the singles who are out having fun and living fulfilled lives are more magnetic and attract the best partners!

Media is exactly the same. Time and time again over the last twenty years, I've witnessed bloggers, authors, speakers, bands and artists who focus on building their own platforms, creating incredible content and nurturing their communities. No matter how small they start, they're the ones who always end up growing a big beautiful buzz around them, which naturally attracts media attention, publishers, record companies and event promoters.

There's that magic moment when the media sees you flourishing, having fun and growing **without them**. The fact that you **don't need them**, draws them to you as they decide they **want a piece of that**. This is the secret to getting top media opportunities, book deals, speaking gigs, and respect from your peers and industry.

Media strategy can be broken down into four pillars: owned, shared, earned and paid:

> **Owned media** *is the media you own outright and control completely, including your blog, website, podcasts, videos, your own magazine and especially your email list.*
> **Shared media** *is social media, which should not be confused with owned media, because you do not own the content.*

> **Earned media** *is coverage and editorial in magazines, on TV, radio or well-known blogs.*
> **Paid media** *typically is advertising.*

Instead of focusing on external people, platforms and media to help you, I recommend spending most of your time honing your craft and creating an abundant, useful, inclusive space with your blogs, ebooks or emails, building your own media empire. That means putting most of your energy into those 'owned' media, instead of waiting or begging other people for a leg up.

Stop waiting for someone else to save you or lift you into the spotlight. Create your own spotlight! And always remember to 'be so good they can't ignore you.'

THE IMPORTANCE OF ONLINE

If you're going to create your own spotlight, you'll need to create your own media platforms. And where better to do that than online? The digital platforms we'll be covering in this chapter include your website and opt-in, blogging, email, webinars, podcasts and social media. All of these, apart from social media, are types of content that you can own forevermore.

And it's oh-so-necessary to create a platform for your business. Your platform is where your audience sees, hears and connects with you. Where you freely share your ideas and inspiration. Having your own platform is essential for getting your message to the world. You might have the best ideas, incredible products and be an expert in your field but, without a platform, you'll never reach your true audience potential.

It's not always geniuses who grow the most abundant audiences. It's the go-getters who do. This does not mean you need to become overly extroverted and be everywhere overnight. Even if you only have five people on your email list, you can create something so incredibly useful that those recipients can't help but share with their friends. This is how you'll radiate that generous, abundant and fulfilled energy ... the kind that people can feel through their screens!

Soulfully select what feels good for you, then action it consistently and authentically. The present and future success of digital engagement is on platforms that are consistent and authentic.

This is how you, as a Soulpreneur, can rise through the **perceived** crowded marketplace. We live in an exciting era for Soulpreneurs, where you don't need to be on TV or on the front of a magazine to share your light with the world.

What's more, you can grow a digital platform without the need for PR teams, book publishers or event promoters. In fact, many of these teams and professionals constantly search the web to **discover** their next breakthrough author, artist or expert for a TV segment. These days, a web presence is non-negotiable!

To get your platform up and running, you may require a web developer or virtual assistant to help you take action, although most steps can be learnt and implemented easily. Your first decision will be whether to take the DIY approach or designate a budget to get professional assistance. From there, you can make it as big as you desire.

Don't worry if any of the following suggestions aren't right for you or your business right now, or in the future. You don't have to do it all. Just skip the ones that don't resonate, depending where you are in your business.

YOUR WEBSITE

Yes, your website is an important part of your business. Just remember, as you go through this section, to not get trapped in perfectionism. By the time your website is perfect, chances are you'll have evolved and be ready for a refresh. It's never-ending, so just get started!

First up, let's clarify the intention of your site. Is it going to be a big interactive business card, a blogging platform, an ecommerce store, a membership site or all of the above? Decide its purpose.

Now, what actions do you want visitors to take, when they visit your website? Do you want them to sign up for your email list, listen to your podcast, read your blog posts, buy tickets and products, or send you an email?

Once the purpose and one main action are decided, these are the elements you'll need to create your website:

Aligned domain name

Securing the exact domain name you desire is getting trickier these days, but don't let that deter you. Ideally, buy your own name and the name of your project or business as domain names. I am fortunate to have soulpreneurs.com and yvetteluciano.com, although I could never find earthevents.com available for anything less than $20,000! We used earthevents.com.au and earthhq.co without any issues.

Professional photos

Do you need professional photos taken? Who could do these for you? Collect references and research local photographers in your price range. Professional photos are a must!

Easy navigation

Keep it nice and easy for your website visitors to navigate their way around your website and to effortlessly find exactly what they are looking for. Simplicity is best.

Fonts and colours

Choose a design that aligns with your brand, as determined in the previous chapter.

Awesome content

While a fancy website might impress your visitor and give a great first impression, it's the useful and engaging content that will ensure your visitors hang around and return. This is much more important than a fancy design. Again, decide whether you will do this yourself or need a copywriter to help you.

Glowing testimonials

Social proof speaks volumes. Your visitors will be drawn in deeper, after reading or watching rave reviews from previous and existing clients.

Why, who, what ... in that order

The information your website must convey are the 3Ws: **why** you do what you do, **who** you do it for and **what** exactly you provide. Sounds obvious, but you'd be surprised how often these basics are missing from new websites.

Mobile responsiveness

Many visitors will access your site via their phone.

Stickiness

Chances are that you have worked hard to get your website visitors to drop by, so let's ensure they stick around! How can you keep visitors on your site? Make sure you're not sending them elsewhere with web links and social media links. If you do need to share external links, make sure they open in new windows.

Easy-to-use ecommerce

Will you be selling products on your site? If so, the check-out process must be user-friendly for your customers. You can research platforms like Shopify, which many start-up Soulpreneurs use with ease.

Actionable opt-in

The most tried and tested way to attract website visitors onto your email list is to give away something super helpful and valuable.

All this may be a lot to figure out in one go, which is why you may wish to hire a developer or, if you're not yet at that stage, a virtual assistant. Whoever develops or assists in creating your site, make sure you have full control to update the site independently.

When locking in the right developer, always get a quote and delivery terms in writing. And make sure you receive a user manual for your site when it's ready. Remember: **you want total access and control**.

At time of writing, I suggest having your site on wordpress.org, which will give you more control and freedom than wordpress.com, or explore options like Squarespace, Wix or one of the newer website builders to get started.

Finally, your site needs to engage and encourage your audience to take action immediately. That means either signing up for your opt-in, buying something from you, or at least recommending you to a friend, depending on your website intention. Do your market research and beta-test your site, by asking a couple of trusted audience members what they think.

A website visitor needs to become a believer first, buyer second. Here's how you can do that.

OPT-INS

Most visitors won't buy on first visit, so that's why you need an 'opt-in' gift. An opt-in is an enticing part of your home page, where your visitor gives you their email address and permission to email them your updates, promotions and invitations. Your opt-in needs to be clear and take centre stage on your home page, because opting in is one of the most valuable actions a visitor can take.

The visitor is 'paying' you with their email address, which is a valuable exchange and should be treated as such. It's a bit like getting someone's mobile number. It could be the beginning of a lifelong relationship if everything goes well, or disappear into nothing if you don't appreciate it and take action.

Your opt-in gift should also give the visitor a great 'sample' of you. It needs to be interesting enough for your visitor to hand over their email address in exchange. Consider that most people are becoming increasingly cautious about doing this.

Some ideas for opt-ins

You could create an ebook, checklist, audio (meditation, songs, lecture, class), or video (exclusive, instructional, educational). Think about the format your audience would enjoy. Then think about the question or advice you get asked for most. Examples include:

- *a free video class on how to make kombucha*
- *the first chapter of your book*
- *a beginner's audio introduction to meditation*
- *exclusive songs or video from the studio*
- *a mini ebook collection of uplifting blog posts*

Ensure the opt-in form is hooked up with your email system, like MailChimp, Infusionsoft or any other email provider. Find one that feels good and easy to use.

Then deliver your gift through an autoresponder sequence, with caring and considerate correspondence full of gratitude, explaining what to expect in the future. You can even invite them to share the opt-in on social media and with friends.

Leadpages and Launch Effect are options for professional opt-in pages, if your site isn't up to it. Once this web page, opt-in form and sequence is set up, regularly test it to ensure it's all running smoothly.

In the meantime, start to screenshot and file away opt-in and thankyou pages that you notice and love. Have them on hand as a reference when it comes time to create your own.

Now you have the honour of receiving your audience members' email addresses, what happens next? Let's talk about your email community.

YOUR EMAIL COMMUNITY

How lucky are we to live at a time when we can have lists of all the people who want to hear more about us and our offerings? Your email community is the list of people who opted in from your website. They are your leads and/or existing customers.

As with everything in a Soulpreneur's business, your focus here should be on **quality over quantity**. A small list of quality subscribers who are engaged with you is better than a big list of broad subscribers who don't really care about or even open your emails. In fact, an unengaged list can be detrimental, as this can contribute to you landing in spam folders. Also, many email providers charge by number of subscribers these days, so you're wasting money when you send emails to unengaged readers.

Likewise, the idea is for you to send good quality emails, not just loads of them. Short, sweet, simple, concise emails that are easy to action. You don't need to be sending daily or weekly newsletters, if you don't want to. Just pick a frequency that feels good for you.

Weekly is great, if you are prolific and have an abundance of useful insights to share with your audience. Otherwise fortnightly or monthly is ideal for a start. Play with this at first to find your flow. Then make a decision and stick to it.

Subject lines and email content

Good copywriting with clever subject lines is important, when you're thinking about creating a quality experience. In my view, the more personal the better. I'm more likely to open up and engage with emails that feel intimate rather than generalised or corporate. Avoid using the word 'newsletter' in the subject line and instead write a subject line that is relevant to the email. Something intriguing. Something **you** would open.

Check in on the intention of how you want the receiver to feel when your email pops up, when they open it, when they finish reading it. I suggest keeping your emails to less than 30% advertising or promoting products. This is about long-term relationships. Nurture them. Brighten up their day. Inspire them. Help them feel better. Be generous. Give them heaps of love and freebies and info that you've been blogging.

Timing

Select the best time of the day and week to send. Time zones play a part in this and some email providers will let you 'timewarp,' so the emails are received at times that are best for each country's time zone. This means that the email provider allows you to schedule your email to arrive in your recipient's inbox at a particular time of day in their own time zone.

SOULPRENEUR STEPS

Now decide for yourself what your email marketing will look like, by answering these questions in your journal:

> *What frequency will you start with?*
> *Which emails do you love to receive and read?*
> *What subject lines would entice your audience?*
> *What is the best time of day or week for you and your audience?*
> *What feelings are you aiming to evoke in the receiver?*

BLOGGING

Another way to share generously with your audience is blogging. This sets a beautiful tone and nurtures your relationship with your audience, leading them to become customers, who want your products, services or events.

While some may say the glory days of blogging have passed, I believe it's simply evolving, which is exciting! There has never been a better time for you to step up and shine more brightly through blogging.

Thankfully, old-school blog monetisation (trying to attract blog sponsors or advertisers) has come to an end for Soulpreneurs. Rather than advertising or sponsorship for other people's products, your blog is your relationship and profile-builder, which exists to connect, serve and promote **your** products and services.

Don't worry about attracting or pleasing anyone except your intended audience. Just choose a format you're comfortable with and start! What feels natural for you? If you're a writer, write blogs. A natural speaker, record audios. Maybe you feel good presenting? In that case, film videos. Remember audios and videos can be transcribed too.

Whichever format you choose, create a batch if possible. This means setting aside a few hours, days or weeks to create a number of posts. Sometimes you can create six months' worth in a long weekend.

Here are my top tips for blogging:

> *Have patience and persistence. Expect slow, steady, sustainable growth.*
> *Be authentic, honest and emotive. Your audience wants to feel something, to connect with you.*
> *Make sure you don't post private conversations or emails without permission. Change names and profiles if need be. And always disclose affiliates or commercial partnerships. Not only is this moral and ethical practice, it's also a legal requirement in many countries.*
> *Remember to reference the sources, quotations and studies that you're using, to back up any of your writing. Credit any books, blogs and images that you share.*
> *Be Google-friendly. Keep an eye on trending search terms and explore search engine optimisation (SEO).*
> *Have a monthly or yearly content plan, to increase productivity and decrease procrastination.*

SOULPRENEUR STEPS

Start now by coming up with **ten blog posts** that you'd love to create, either written or recorded. Be consistent. Keep the topics and tone on brand and true to you. And have fun with it!

Topic 1: ______________________________.

Topic 2: ______________________________.

Topic 3: ________________________________.

Topic 4: ________________________________.

Topic 5: ________________________________.

Topic 6: ________________________________.

Topic 7: ________________________________.

Topic 8: ________________________________.

Topic 9: ________________________________.

Topic 10: ________________________________.

Blogging is a great way to develop your voice and connect with your audience in an instant. You can share book ideas or song demos along the way. Discovering what resonates with your audience will give you an abundance of new product or service ideas, as well as valuable feedback.

SOCIAL MEDIA

As owned media, your website and email list make up the core of the media that you control. Social media, on the other hand, is shared media and not owned by you. Instead, it can be viewed as an excellent connection and promotional tool, but not on a level with the platforms we have already discussed, because different social media platforms will come and go, changing throughout your career.

Social media can become a bright shiny object in your business and daily life—extremely distracting and perfect for procrastination. However, when used mindfully and with clear intentions, it can be lots of fun and one of the best marketing and promotional tools we are blessed with today.

From a business perspective, your intention for being on social media is to grow your audience, and drive your followers to your website and opt-in. This is why your digital home needs to be linked everywhere on your social media profiles.

Social media is such a large topic. It's evolving and updating every day, and it's too far beyond the scope of this book to go into great detail. However, we'll cover the 'need to knows,' to ensure you're on the right track and not too overwhelmed or concerned about this sensitive topic.

Let's use the analogy that if the online world were real life, social media would be the 'cocktail party.' It's a place to go and mingle, but it's not **your** house. The host could cut the party short, enforce new rules or kick people out at any time.

Your role at the cocktail party is to connect with people, to spark a genuine relationship. That conversation then goes back to your place—or your website in the online world—as you get to know each other better and stay in touch. Then you can catch up with those people anytime, without leaving it all in the hands of the cocktail party host to organise another meet-up.

Starting out

Strategy is helpful with social media, but just have a play when you're first starting out. Get to know how and why your audience is there, then think about and implement a strategy later.

There are so, so many platforms to test. At time of writing, it's Facebook, Instagram, Twitter, Pinterest, Google+, LinkedIn and YouTube. I could go on! Chances are there will be even more new platforms by the time you read this book.

Yes, it's great to dip your toe in, try them all, and then pick a few that feel good for you. Probably, the platforms you enjoy are the ones your audience loves too.

The great news is that you don't need to do them all. Just like you can't accept every social invitation in life and will graciously decline a few, you need to find peace (not FOMO), in your decision not to be on certain social media platforms. Consider your audience. Feel into what they want and which platform they prefer. Explore where they are active. Select the best and move away from the rest.

SOULPRENEUR STEPS

Take some notes on **how you'll use social media** by doing market research and answering these questions:

> *Which social media platforms do you enjoy, and why?*
> *Which social media platforms do you feel your audience loves, and why?*
> *Which new social media platforms will you explore?*
> *Which social media platforms will you stop using?*

How much time will you spend on social media each day?

....

....

....

....

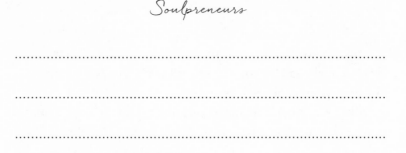

STRATEGY SUGGESTIONS

Once you have selected your social media platforms of choice, here are some tips to help you have fun growing your fans, followers and friends:

- *Think like a publisher, not a promoter. Try this ratio for posting: 50% original content like thoughts, photos, blog posts, videos; 40% sharing other people's content and engaging; 10% promoting and selling your products and services.*
- *Be consistent but chilled. Less is more. Don't oversaturate.*
- *Always post yourself if you are a personal brand. If your team ever posts on your behalf, make sure it's clear that it's not you. To do this, you could use a team name, like: The Sally Smith Team, Team Delta, etc.*
- *You can pre-schedule your posts through a provider like Hootsuite, but be available and present to engage with comments. Interactions with your audience on social media need to be consistent with your brand. It's especially important to have guidelines in place when you have a team.*
- *Also important is having a policy in place for robots, and using a consistent approach to negative commenters. Please remember that you may attract troublemakers or negativity the more you grow, and that's okay.*
- *Select relevant aligned hashtags, and don't go overboard.*

- *Use these hashtags to find and comment on others' posts about you. If they care enough to take the time to post about you, it's considerate to acknowledge them.*
- *Create consistent images with the colours and fonts of your brand.*
- *Check the guidelines of the social media platform, to ensure you're using it correctly.*
- *Expect slow, sustainable growth on social media.*
- *Don't believe the hype of viral sensations. We can all hope to manifest viral success, but we can't plan it strategically. Focus on creating content that people will naturally want to share and watch the miracle unfold … fingers crossed!*
- *Create a profile with your business or brand name on all platforms, just in case you change your mind about which ones you want to use. And if you aren't enjoying a platform, take a break or try another.*
- *And as with everything, keep perspective and don't take it too seriously.*

OTHER MEDIA TO CHECK OUT

Webinars

Webinars are digital classes where your audience can listen to or see you live, by watching a video or slideshow, with you taking questions by chat or live call.

Webinars or Live interactive videos are a great way to share free information, engage with your audience and test out ideas for courses and larger products. They are also great for launching new products. The webinar can be your product launch party!

Summits

An online summit is a series of audios or videos on a topic or theme, with different experts delivering classes through a specific period. These are usually free for your audience throughout the week(s) of the summit, but if they want to download the content or listen back later, they usually have to purchase all of the content as a bundle.

You may encourage the guest experts to be affiliates, which will allow them to promote to their audiences, and increase sign-ups and engagement.

Podcasts

Podcasts are hosted or streamed audio recordings, delivered through streaming services and also shared from your site. The format of the content can be just you talking and sharing ideas, or interviews with other people aligned with your audience. Episodes can be any length, and while twenty to thirty minutes has been suggested as the best length, you know your audience best.

Podcasts are great for busy people, who can listen through their phone on their way to work, cooking for the kids, or on a morning walk.

~ SOULPRENEUR SUCCESS SUMMARY ~

✓ *Decide on the main purpose of your website.*

✓ *Secure your chosen domain name.*

✓ *Research platforms and ecommerce.*

✓ *Make a decision about DIY or hiring a developer.*

✓ *Get your design, images, photos and any other visuals together.*

✓ *Write the content for your site.*

✓ *Choose your ecommerce provider, if you need one.*

✓ *Create a valuable opt-in gift and link it to an email marketing list.*

✓ *Write consistent and authentic emails to those who have opted into your list.*

✓ *Make a list of blog topics or a content plan, then batch your content creation.*

✓ *Research where your audience likes to hang out on social media.*

✓ *Play on social media first, then make a strategy later.*

chapter SIXTEEN

PR, Media and Positive Influencers

Publicity is absolutely critical.
A good PR story is infinitely more
effective than a front page ad.

– **Richard Branson**

If you're just starting out with the help of this book, your business may not necessarily be ready for mass media. When it is though, this chapter will be here for you!

While your marketing is focused on what **you** want to say and how you want to say it, your PR is more about what **others** say about you. This especially includes your peers and influencers in your industry, as it's about creating long-lasting relationships. You can implement this right now, regardless of where you are in your business.

Client and customer testimonials and rave reviews can become your most powerful PR. Social media platforms have given us the power to become promotional outlets for all the people and products we love. We have become part of the new bigger, wider media landscape.

While the media world is evolving faster right now than ever, let's check in on where we've been and where we are going.

MEDIA, PROMO AND PUBLICITY

'Media' is typically defined as mass communication of a message. All forms of media are wide-reaching communication channels, with the purpose of raising awareness and influencing people to buy or believe in something.

In your business and life, you might hear media being defined as traditional or digital media, traditional being broadcast (television, radio) and print (newspapers, magazines), and digital being blogs, online news sites, email, websites and podcasts. If you're new to this world, you may find there's a lot of terminology used in the earned media world. Simple words like media, PR, promo, publicity, marketing and communications can seem to all blur into one, which can make it challenging to know what you need.

When I refer to 'media' throughout this chapter, the term will encompass anyone you may want to approach, including traditional and digital media, television and magazines, bloggers and influencers. How do you know which outlet you need? Well, let's start with a few definitions.

PR stands for public relations, which is essentially the communication and relationship between a brand and the world. The aim of all PR is to inform people about a person or product and inspire them to take action, usually buy something (a book or event ticket or product) or believe in something. Some PR is focused solely on swaying the public perception on a particular person or topic.

If your marketing was an umbrella covering branding, media platforms, books and speaking, I would see PR as a significant part of that marketing effort, not separate from it.

Underneath the PR heading, you have:

- **Publicity:** media coverage and exposure (aiming for public attention)
- **Promotion:** any means of informing people of your product in a way that inspires them to buy, including publicity, product sampling etc.
- **Media relations:** managing the relationship, correspondence and conversations with media
- **Influencer engagement:** bloggers or celebrities sharing and promoting your products and services
- **Crisis management:** for when you attract unexpected coverage that you want handled with grace and positivity

GO PRO OR DO IT YOURSELF?

When starting out, you can take a DIY approach with everything except publicity and crisis management. For those, there are PR companies you can hire, often for upwards of $3,000 per month on three-month retainers. (Many of the best are two or three times that investment.) Given the expense of this route, I encourage you to be open to learning and making the right decision about hiring a professional or doing it yourself.

So let's start by weighing up why we need media coverage at all. There are two main reasons:

1. To attract a new audience to your own platform.
2. To increase your social proof, because the audience's perception is that something is good when it's on TV or in a magazine.

Once you've made the decision on whether this is important for you at your stage of business, it's time to decide if you'll be doing it yourself or getting a professional in. The benefits of hiring a professional are that they will create an awesome strategy, write media releases, brainstorm angles, pitch to media, leverage their contacts, and organise interviews and coverage for you. The downside is that sometimes it isn't always worth the significant investment. You have to consider the objective and return on investment, because coverage doesn't always convert to sales or sign-ups.

Luckily, the media world has changed and hiring a professional isn't the only route. It's never been easier or more affordable to put together a great media kit and campaign. You will save significant money doing it yourself, although you will invest time, and lots of it.

Either way, media coverage can be a highly-influential marketing and promotional tool. It's relatively inexpensive in comparison to paid media and appears to be more influential. PR pros will tell you media coverage is worth three times the expense of paid media. Not to mention brand ambassadors, bloggers and influencers, who are becoming far more important than print and broadcast journalists. I believe that's because 'word of mouth' is at play.

People are more likely to buy if someone they trust, love and follow is supporting the product, especially if they have a reputation for being authentic and only sharing with integrity.

RELATIONSHIPS WITH THE MEDIA

You will need to earn all media coverage through strong relationships, connections, engaging angles and, most importantly, a product or service that media can't help but share!

Keep your communications concise and considerate. Chances are that the journalists, bloggers and influencers on your wish list are busy people. You are one of hundreds or thousands of publicists reaching out to them wanting coverage, so stay focused on **what's in it for them**. Make it clear how you can help them.

It's important to remember that influencer and journalist relationships can take time. Maybe the person you reach out to can't come to a particular event or share your book on Instagram this time. But if you are courteous, maybe they will next time.

And remember, it's beyond your control what the media says about you and when.

SOULPRENEUR STEPS

It's time to get clear on your **'who and why'** in media.

Who *are the media outlets or influencers you want coverage with and why? Create a clear list of your media targets, including all the magazines, TV or radio shows, podcasts, blogs and websites that you feel have an audience that needs your message.*

....

....

....

....

Why *would they love to hear from you?*

....

....

....

....

CREATE YOUR OWN CAMPAIGN

Follow these steps and create a campaign to send to the above media targets.

Step 1: Why are you doing the campaign? Clarify the campaign's purpose and intention. Are you bringing awareness to a new event, product or issue, or are you trying to influence public perception about something?

Step 2: Next, set your goals, remembering to keep them specific, measurable and attainable, such as quantity of placements, quality of engagement, target sales or increase in business growth.

Step 3: Decide on the target audience. Who are the readers, viewers and listeners you want to reach?

Step 4: List all of the media outlets your audience consumes. Do some research and ask your audience, if you aren't sure.

Step 5: Craft your key messages, making sure you don't have too many. A few is plenty. Simplicity is key. It can be as simple as a new book coming out, an event going on sale, or a product being released.

Step 6: Form a strategy, specifying how you will achieve your objectives. Then go on to design the methods you will use, including specific actions, tasks, deadlines and budgets for each item.

Once your campaign is complete, reflect on what was worthwhile, what wasn't and what you will do even better next time.

STRATEGIES AND METHODS

You might be wondering what strategies and methods you can use, so let's get more specific. Here are some tips for creating a media strategy.

First, you must know your media. Familiarise yourself with every magazine, blog or influencer that your audience respects. Read or listen to them inside out. You can take it at your own pace, checking out a few new blogs and magazines a week to get started.

Then it's time to start engaging. Follow the journalists, outlets or influencers on social media, comment on their posts, share their articles and show your support. If it's a blogger you're pitching to and they have speaking gigs, go see them. Nothing beats a person-to-person interaction. Volunteer for them. Do whatever it takes, though always with respect, consideration and realistic expectations.

Pitching

> *Get personal in your pitch. Don't send a mass email. Ever. Please!*
> *On the rare occasion you need to get your media release to every single outlet quickly, you may choose a paid mass distribution service for widespread media placements and syndication.*
> *Keep your pitch clear and concise. An intriguing email subject, a couple of short paragraphs, a few bullet points and (occasionally) a one-page media release attachment is more than enough.*
> *Do the work for them. They are busy! Offer them suggested questions to ask you. Tell them what's in it for them. Say how you serve their audience.*

Engaging angles

These are the four most engaging angles, which can grab attention and get you mentioned. Consider them when you're creating your pitch.

1. **What's big news?** What's currently trending? What expertise or experience can you share about these hot topics?
2. **What stories, surveys or statistics back up your pitch?** Do you need to create your own survey?
3. **What are the breaking developments?** New exclusive info is great for journalists, who love being the trendsetters and sharing original content.
4. **Controversy, disaster and drama** are all attention grabbers, especially in mainstream media. As a Soulpreneur, be mindful of your sensitivity and attracting negativity or attention that you can't handle. For Soulpreneurs, not 'all publicity is good publicity,' so protect your wellbeing and make conscious intuitive decisions about where to draw the line.

Media releases

Good old media releases are not the almighty and powerful tools they once were, as there are so many ways to send and receive promotional messages and material. However, for those who would love to receive your info, here's a clear, concise and simple structure suggestion for your media release (from top to bottom of page):

> *Banner or image*
> *Date and embargo, if required*
> *Media release headline in title case*
> *Subheadings, so you can keep your headline short and punchy*
> *Bullet points*

- *Amazing opening line that summarises the announcement in the release. Hook them immediately, then get to the facts*
- *Enough info for your target to write a post or story, but keep under 500 words*
- *Quotes, facts and stats; they give your target their article instantly*
- *Spellcheck. Typo check. Double-check facts and stats*
- *Second person to read through*
- *'Boilerplate' or succinct paragraph, summarising the person or company*
- *All contact details including name, email and phone contacts*
- *Additional Q&A document or fast facts*
- *High-res professional photos and two bios (a one-page and a one-para) on standby*

You can view an example of a media release here: **yvetteluciano.com/bookclub**

A NOTE ON RELATIONSHIPS IN YOUR INDUSTRY AND WITH INFLUENCERS

The best way to receive support within your industry is by establishing long-term relationships. The keyword here is 'genuine.'

When you see a leader of your industry receiving an abundance of support from their peers and others in their industry, it mostly comes down to a real relationship and respect that has been built over many years. This cannot be bought or influenced by money or even the most powerful publicity.

How do you create long-term relationships and respect in your industry? It's very simple and straightforward: simply be a good person. Be respected and known as someone who supports others and your industry in general. Make this a way of life, not a marketing strategy. Be supportive, be helpful and be detached from the outcome of what these friendships with do for your business.

Do not use people, suck up to people or fake your desire for a real friendship. People can feel it, they can tell.

Simply be you, be real and be grateful for any support you receive on others' platforms. And remove any expectations or entitlements from the business rewards of these relationships.

~ SOULPRENEUR SUCCESS SUMMARY ~

✓ *Consider where your business is at.*

✓ *Decide what sort of media you need right now.*

✓ *Make the decision on hiring an expert or learning about it yourself.*

✓ *Explore where you would like to be seen.*

✓ *Design your campaign.*

✓ *Pitch and deliver.*

chapter SEVENTEEN

Writing and Speaking with the World

Find your voice and inspire others to find theirs.
– Stephen Covey

One of the most powerful ways to share your message and your light is through writing books and speaking at events. Communicating and sharing with your audience directly.

You don't need to be a natural-born writer or speaker; most of your favourite authors and teachers developed their art and communication skills through courses and coaching, although mostly through practice. Just get out there, get started. Don't wait until you're perfect. Every practice book will get better, every practice speaking gig will improve.

Let's now explore how to share the light and the story within you with the world. We've been waiting to hear from you!

BOOKS AND EBOOKS

For Soulpreneurs, writing a book to accompany your business normally means non-fiction and personal development style which is what I'll base this guidance on. However, most of this information will be helpful regardless of the type of book you wish to release into the world.

Why release a book at all?

1. Your book can position you as an expert.
2. It's an awesome 'business card.'
3. It's a fantastic anchor for your courses, workshops and other products.
4. It's the perfect way to share your message with the world.

The exciting part is that there's never been an easier time to release books, thanks to the self-publishing opportunities of the digital world. With the vast majority of books now sold online, it's empowering to know you don't need a publisher for your book to be available on digital bookstores like Amazon, Book Depository, Kindle or iBooks. Just ensure that you make the right decision for you and your book.

WRITING AND CREATING YOUR BOOK

Getting all those wonderful ideas, stories and messages out of your head and into a book is the most fun, yet overwhelming part. Even if you have a natural love of writing, it's pretty daunting. Not only have I helped other authors through this journey, but I've been on the other side, writing *Learn to Thrive* and now *Soulpreneurs* for you. In the author seat, you may sway from the exhilarating excitement about your book and writing to sudden fear and overwhelm.

One of my favourite creatives SARK writes: *Your inner critics will follow you into the writing cave.* Your self-belief will be tested like crazy during the process of writing your book, but after everything you've experienced in your life, career and business, I know you can do this.

And I know the world needs your book. Can you imagine the powerful impact that your book will have on even just one person? That in itself is why you need to do this. Even if your book is your personal journey, it has a message to share with your readers.

Here are some ideas for working through writer's block:

> *Increase your daily spiritual practice.*
> *Spend more time with other creatives and risk-takers.*
> *Pray to your spiritual guides and Archangel Gabriel, the carer of writers and communicators.*
> *Reflect on why you want to create a book.*

Outline

Take a look at similar books in your genre to see how they are laid out. Here is a list of the sections in a book. You may wish to group your chapters together, so that your book has two, three or four parts.

> *Dedication*
> *Testimonials*
> *Contents*
> *Foreword*
> *Preface*
> *Introduction*
> *Chapters*
> *Closing notes*

> *Recommended resources*
> *Acknowledgements*
> *About the author*

Team

These are the people who will help bring your book to life. It may be just one person, an awesome friend, or great professionals:

- **Book agent**—a professional who is well-connected in the industry.

  Your book agent manages most of your publisher correspondence, negotiations and overall writing career. They usually get paid around 15-25% of your book royalties and payments. A great agent can do wonders for your book and career; a crappy one can do more damage than good, so be discerning.

  If you're set on going with a major publishing house, it's highly recommended that you have an agent. Most publishing companies will not accept proposals and submissions from authors without one. If you're self-publishing, an agent isn't particularly necessary.
- **Book editor**—a professional who helps with the book-writing process.

  There are different kinds of editors and what you need will depend on your skill set. An editor may help with any detail of the book-writing process, from your outline, structure and research, to tone, voice, messaging and language. An editor can also proofread your book, and I strongly advise that you have a professional proofreader triple-checking for grammar, spelling and typos. In my view, editors are worth every cent. They enhance the quality and richness of your words and overall book. Even if you're a natural writer or have already done extensive research, I believe you need at least one person other than yourself guiding you through the book-writing process.

Those are the main people on your book team, but you also may consider:

- **Researcher**—to help you fact check and collect case studies.
- **Ghostwriter or copywriter**—to write some or all of your book. (This may seem like a quick and easy way to get your book out there, but think it through carefully before exploring this option.)
- **Beta readers**—your 'test reading' team, usually made up of your existing audience or peers, to read your book drafts and give feedback at times along the way.

If you are self-publishing, you will also need:

- **Book designer**
- **Typesetter**
- **Printer**
- **Distributor**

It's up to you or your agent to get you onto the digital platforms. If you're lucky enough to have a distributor, they will get you into physical bookstores. If you don't, you can approach them individually. In all circumstances, I recommend you consider a book publicist.

If you discuss sensitive topics, health or dietary recommendations or personal stories about people or clients, I recommend having a lawyer take a look at your book.

And finally, if you refer to anyone within your book, get their permission in writing. Alternatively, change their names and identities and disclose that fact at the start.

SOULPRENEUR STEPS

Let's get clear on **what** you'll be writing and **why**, by looking at these questions and then writing any reactions/responses below:

> *Why do you feel the call?*
> *What are the topics and themes you want to write about?*
> *What are the possible book titles and subtitles?*

....

....

....

....

....

....

Write blog posts to test topics and themes and see what resonates with your audience and lights you up. Research topics and themes on Amazon or Google and see which ones are aligned with your area of interest, expertise or experience. Stick to topics and themes you know and check thoroughly with other professionals or existing research that what you're teaching is up-to-the-minute industry best practice.

- *Who are you writing for?*
- *What are the core messages of your book?*
- *What is your legacy? What do you wish to hand down to the generations?*
- *What similar books or authors are available?*
- *What do you envision as the book cover?*
- *What are the trends in your genre?*

....

....

....

....

....

....

People do tend to judge a book by its cover. It can make or break the sale. The cover sets the tone and vibe, so ensure your audience would be proud to be seen holding the book you're producing. Imagine them showing it off on Instagram! And remember that your branding needs to be in alignment.

- *Will you record an audiobook?*
- *Do you intend to release accompanying products?*
- *When is your deadline?*

....

....

....

....

....

....

Note that a major publishing house loves to have the book sitting in their warehouse months before release, whereas a self-publishing author may have books arriving on their doorstep just days before release.

RELEASING YOUR BOOK

You have two options for releasing your book: self-publishing or with a traditional publishing house. Both have pros and cons, which I'll summarise here. Please note, this advice is general.

I suggest to all first-time authors that you self-publish your first book, even if it's just a digital ebook, because it helps you figure out your place in the market and navigate book publishing. It also means that you have a place to start from when approaching or negotiating with agents or publishers. If they can see you have already self-published a book with even a couple of thousand sales, they will take you more seriously than if you haven't yet released anything.

Self-publishing

Now is the best time in history to self-publish, with opportunities like crowdfunding to help with production and printing costs, and print-on-demand services like CreateSpace meaning you don't have to hold stock, because the book is printed and shipped to your reader directly. Of course, you can always do digital ebooks, removing the need for printing completely. Either way, you will receive a larger payment per book from self-publishing.

Traditional publishing

As previously mentioned, you will generally need a book or literary agent to pitch to publishers, as well as a book proposal. Most publishers are looking for authors who have:

> *A fresh twist on a popular topic*
> *An existing audience, platform and reach*

The authors who attract the best deals are the ones who are already out in the world sharing their work, and selling their own books, products and services with proven success and interest.

When you're offered a book deal, it's usually accompanied by a book advance, essentially a loan against book royalties. First-time authors may be offered anything from a $3,000 advance to a six-figure sum. The deal will also specify how often you'll receive royalties and the percentage of sales.

I'm sure you are starting to see why being an author means becoming entrepreneurial, as you can rarely make an abundant living from book sales alone.

PROMOTING YOUR BOOK

Regardless of which publishing route your book takes to arrive in the world, it's your responsibility as the author to market and promote your book. Gone are the days when publishing houses invested serious time and money into book PR. Their job is getting your book into stores and onto shelves. They see your job as getting out there and driving people to pick up a copy.

Go back to the chapters on marketing, promotion and PR to come up with your book marketing strategy. In this section, we will look only at book-specific promo tips. The most important point to remember is that marketing starts before the book release. In addition:

> *Take your audience on the book-writing journey. Make them feel part of it and build the anticipation.*
> *Send the book to influencers, bloggers, peers and media, weeks or months before the release.*
> *Create a hashtag and activate social media buzz.*
> *Drive a pre-order campaign and offer bonus bundles with audios, event tickets or other exciting products that align with your core messages.*
> *Create a big launch day impact!*
> *Create a book trailer or video series, with insight and extra information on book background or topics.*
> *Share more about your personal journey with the book, its creation and why you are releasing it.*
> *Host book events or store signings for in-person impact.*

SPEAKING WITH THE WORLD

Have a think about your experiences of watching speakers. Is there anything more powerful than being in a room with like-minded people, sharing an experience with your favourite speaker or performer?

One of the things I love most about live experiences is that they are direct and potent. You ignite change in your audience's life. Plus, live events are fun!

Whether you want to rise up as a speaker, host events or workshops, or even speak with your audience through video, I hope to give you the confidence to move through your public speaking fears and more clarity on how to craft your talks and lever up your presenting. Because speaking is so influential!

Public speaking

When your audience comes to your event or workshop, they are actively engaging with your brand. They have entered your world for the duration of the event, so you want to make sure it's memorable for the right reasons. Your audience get the full experience of you and your brand. It's experiential marketing at its finest. They receive the full energy of you and the other members of your audience. The sights, smells, sounds, taste and feel of your brand.

I used to think that there was no way on earth I would get up onstage and speak by choice, or lead workshops, or group coaching calls, or speak on camera. But the moment I stepped out of my own way and focused more on the audience, my fear started to shift.

I still get nervous and don't feel so comfortable speaking with large groups, but I am far too devoted to my message to let that get in my way. And like everything in our businesses and lives, the more we do something, the more comfortable we become.

Always remember it's not about you. It's about your message and your audience. You are just the delivery person. Focus on your message. Focus on the person receiving it.

Talking on stage or on camera isn't for everyone and isn't compulsory for Soulpreneurs. Be real with yourself. Ensure it feels aligned with your soul and purpose. If you find you have no desire to ever speak with an audience, just skip it altogether.

SOULPRENEUR STEPS

Now is your chance to gain a little insight, if you have the slightest calling.

> *What are the first feelings that come to mind, when you think about public speaking?*
> *Why do you think these feelings arise?*
> *What are your fears and where do they come from?*
> *What exactly about public speaking makes you fearful?*
> *What can you do to help move through these fears?*
For example: increasing your spiritual practice, hypnotherapy, kinesiology, journalling through your fears, deep visualisations of yourself onstage delivering an awesome talk, or filming a life-changing video that your audience loves
> *What excites you about the idea of speaking and sharing your message?*
> *What exactly is the message that you want to share?*
For example: your personal story, lessons, educational and informational content
> *Will you be creating anything to help deliver your content?*
> *What are the core facts you want to share?*
> *Will you be delivering your message on stage or on camera?*
If onstage, what types of stages and events? If on camera, how will you record and deliver your videos or content?

Take time now to brainstorm your ideas for your talks and topics, and core lessons or information you wish to share. Then dive into the delivery.

....

....

....

....

....

....

....

....

....

....

....

....

If you're serious about a speaking career, you could hire a professional one-on-one speaking coach.

Additionally, event promotors will want to see you have experience (via a show reel or clip) and an existing audience, and that you can create your own buzz. If it's a publicly-ticketed event, they need to feel confident your audience will attend. It's a little different with corporate gigs or other speaking opportunities, when you are hired by an organisation to come and talk about your specific area of expertise or experience.

Build your confidence and develop your speaking skills. Start small and start free!

CRAFTING AND DELIVERING AN ENGAGING TALK

To be engaging, it's imperative that you customise your talks, hooks and angles to the audience you are speaking for. Always be **100% you.** Just ensure you use stories and examples that the audience will relate to.

This will require clarity around your audience. If it's your event, then you'll already be clear on who they are from the work you've done earlier. If it's someone else's event or vlog, ask the host for a full understanding of the audience demographics, size, interests and desires.

Researching and familiarising yourself with the audience you're addressing is non-negotiable when crafting your engaging talk, but there's much more to it than that. From working with the most professional speakers out there to moving into speaking myself, I've found five core components of the best talks:

1. Connection
2. Hook
3. Journey
4. Lesson
5. Call to action

These components will help you structure your talk into an intro, main body and conclusion.

Connection

Always approach a talk with the intention to connect rather than impress your audience. You are there to inform or inspire in an entertaining way. Do they feel your presence? Do they feel they can trust you? Do they feel intrigued by what you have to say?

Here are some tips to connect with your audience.

> *Talk* **with** *them, not at them. Help them feel part of the conversation.*
> *Make eye contact.*
> *Keep a steady talking speed.*
> *Breathe! Even encourage your audience to go through some breathing or do a short meditation, if that aligns with your messaging.*
> *Keep it simple.*
> *Don't use industry jargon or fancy big words that you wouldn't use in normal conversation.*
> *Be honest. If you're obviously nervous, such as shaking or stumbling over words, acknowledge it with humour, then move on quickly.*
> *Tell them how important this opportunity to speak with this audience is to you. If you are excited to be there and passionate about your message, it will help the audience feel the same way. If your audience don't feel you care about them, they will find it hard to care about you and your message.*
> *Get clear on how you want your audience to feel.*
> *Don't show off! It's okay to share ten years of experience of harmful chemicals because you want your audience to take a stand for the environment. It's not okay to be some superior brainiac. Share only what is relevant and interesting to the audience's lives, interests, dreams and desires.*
> *Be comfortable to pause with presence and power.*

> *Practise your talk with someone who will give you gentle, constructive feedback. And watch videos of great speakers to study what you like about their style. (TED talks are perfect for this!)*
> *Try not to read from scripts, but have points or anchor words on cards that will pull you back into your message and ensure you don't forget anything important. And include your pauses and body cues.*
> *Be respectful of your audience's time. Don't run over or under.*
> *Thank your host, event producer and audience.*
> *And smile!*

In my band days, my dad always said, 'Smile when you're on stage. It's human instinct for us to smile back when someone is smiling at us.' So breathe. Smile. Be yourself. Believe in yourself.

You've got this! You are worthy of being seen and heard. The world needs your voice.

Hook

Your hook is the crux of your talk and ties into the purpose of speaking to this audience. It is usually the opener, which sets the tone and theme. And you want to start strong!

Whether it's an attention-grabbing statistic or a funny story, you've got to get your audience on side right from the beginning. Get clear on your hook, then build your talk around it.

Talk about what you know, because the more you know your topic, the more natural you will be. Think about what topic you're comfortable speaking about and what you want your audience to remember you for. This is your hook and the message you want to reiterate throughout your talk.

Your audience needs to know the purpose of your talk, so make it clear from the beginning: *I'm here to share the lessons I've learnt in my experience with [...............] to help you on your journey.*

Your hook not only captures attention, clarifies the purpose of your talk and creates an anchor, it will make it clear to your audience whether your objective is to inspire, comfort or inform.

Journey

Your stories will make your message memorable. Taking your audience on a journey is the whole point. A good reference point is 'the hero's journey' discussed earlier, which I recommend applying to storytelling throughout all your talks, books and blogs. The 'journey' should be intentional and follow a path to a destination.

Here's how the flow might go:

> *Set up the journey in your introduction. Start in a place that the audience recognises and has connection, a place they can see and feel safe.*
> *The call to adventure begins, the moment of 'crisis'—whatever that may be for you.*
> *Then comes the wake-up call.*
> *Take them through the challenges, changes and discoveries which led to the transformation. The audience is here to receive your discoveries, your lessons. These lessons tie into your hook, your theme, your talk's purpose.*
> *Close with a call to action.*

When sharing personal anecdotes, remember to include your 'who, when, where and what.' Use specific descriptive details to set the scene, particularly at the peak moment of your story. Know when to dive into detail, without overdosing on narrative.

It's important to take your audience on an emotional journey too, because emotive talks are engaging talks. Keep in mind that you want to start and finish with hope, inspiration and humour, if possible. Consider including metaphors, analogies, surprise and proverbs.

Consider the clarity of your transitions, using phrases like: 'This leads to ...' or 'The lesson here is ...' or 'Fast forward ten years ...'

Keep it short and sweet. While you're developing your speaking confidence, keep to a concise twenty minutes. This is much more powerful than a drawn-out hour. Leave them wanting more.

Lesson

The lessons are the gold throughout your journey. They speak to the promise of your hook. They are the reason you are sharing your story with the audience.

You may have one lesson or ten. It doesn't matter, so long as you are clear what you'll share. Keep everything relevant to the lessons.

Every journey needs a destination, a conclusion and a resolution. That's where the lessons live. End strong, recap and drive your lessons home.

Call to action

Once your audience is moved by you and your connection, hooked by what you're sharing, have been on the journey and learnt the lessons, it's time for action.

This is when they say, 'Yes! I'm ready for the next step. Sign me up!' Tell them what happens next and ask them to take action. Leave them inspired and uplifted. Make it crystal clear what they do next.

LAST FEW CONSIDERATIONS ...

Q&A sessions

Be clear with your audience on how this will roll. You may want to hold questions until the end or at dedicated times, so you don't lose your flow. Be mindful that Q&A sessions can make or break the vibe of a room. Make this decision with discernment.

Presentations

You may want to impress your audience with whiz-bang slides, but chances are your audience will have a better time if they feel part of the conversation.

Interaction

If connection with each other is important to your audience, include an exercise that gets them chatting.

Music

The music you play before, during and after will influence the emotion and energy of your talk.

Your speaking career will flourish if you prepare and practise, but my ultimate secret to being a super successful and soulful speaker is this: **be you, be you, be you!**

EVENTS

Hosting events is a massive topic and one I love and know inside out, after almost fifteen years of producing and promoting them for everyone from rock stars to celebrity chefs. As it is such a detailed area of expertise, I couldn't possibly cover in this book every single thing I know about creating events that are soulful and a sell-out. In this section, I'll cover the basic steps to event success.

Many experts in the personal development world have noticed the resurgence of leaders hosting in-person experiences, in favour of online teaching. As Tony Robbins says: *Events are the most fun and fast way to create the deepest impact in people's lives.* Not only do they create impact, but events will grow your audience, influence and income.

Whether it's a social event, spiritual gathering, educational class, seminar, workshop, retreat, product or book launch, community fundraiser or business conference, soulful events that sell out are at the forefront of this resurgence. It's a wise move, because events solve the everyday challenges of Soulpreneurs by:

> *Growing and nurturing your audience*
> *Shining the spotlight on you and your expertise in a noisy digital world*
> *Affirming your expert status*
> *Connecting you with fellow influencers and speakers*
> *Gaining attention and respect from media, publishers and producers*
> *Providing a lucrative income stream*

Events are timeless too. There's no relying on the latest digital trends and strategies, which are hot one day, gone the next. Plus there's the magic and joy of spending real-life time with our beautiful audience and community.

Clarity around the experience

For a Soulpreneur, exploring new ways to serve, engage and communicate with your audience and reach more clients isn't always easy online, which is why I keep coming back to the proven, effective form of marketing that has been around forever ... **experiential marketing**.

We have all been on the receiving end of experiential marketing, whether it be our favourite speaker, teacher or performer, or a life-changing interaction or memory. The **experience** affirmed that person—that brand—as part of your life.

Now, don't let the fact that this was experiential marketing taint the special moment you had, because there's nothing quite like it. And you get this opportunity to create a transformational experience with your audience too.

It's an experience that is not as hard to sell as some people will have you believe; an experience that some Soulpreneurs build their whole business and profile around. And I'll let you in on a little backstage secret. Many of the most profitable and powerful events I've produced have been intimate health retreats and business mastermind days. Bigger isn't always better. I've run twenty-person retreats that have made double the profit of a 1000-attendee seminar.

Marketing your event

Now it may sound obvious, but marketing and branding can all too easily be underestimated or rushed in the busy-ness of managing an event. It's all about timing. Audience anticipation and excitement are crucial for big ticket sales.

Marketing and branding is best planned and rolled out before the event goes on sale. It's not impossible, yet highly challenging, to try to resuscitate the event marketing down the track.

Stress-free organisation and flow

Following the process is key. There is a flow and process required for smooth and successful event organisation. And you must do everything in the right order. Luckily, this is a totally learnable skill, which you'll practise and process.

SOULPRENEUR STEPS

Event success depends on **your intention** and what your **audience are seeking**, so let's get clear right now:

- *Who exactly is your event for?*
- *Who isn't it for?*
- *What is keeping them up at night or stressing them out during the day?*
- *What would they like to experience or know more about that is within your expertise?*
- *Why is the event happening?*
- *Why can the audience not miss it?*

Write down all the different topics and solutions that your events could offer.

> *For example, the crystal-clear solution to your audience's challenge might be learning meditation or cooking, getting moving or working out, connecting with new like-minded people, having a fun night out, or making more money in their business.*

....

....

....

....

....

....

STEPS TO EVENT SUCCESS

There are six steps to event success. They are a proven process which I created and follow. The six steps are:

1. Dream
2. Plan
3. Brand
4. Launch
5. Showtime!
6. Wrap

Dream up the vision

First, you'll want to explore your event vibe, by going back to exactly **why** you're hosting the event and who for. The more specific the better, especially being clear on the audience's challenges and how your event solves those problems. Visualise it all, from what your event is going to be, through what happens, to the location, the venue, the timing—everything!

Clarify the purpose from a profit perspective. Your event may serve a marketing or money-making purpose. You might be using it to grow your audience and want as many attendees as possible, so need to keep ticket prices accessible. You may just want to break even, because the event is a marketing campaign that pays for itself. Or you may want events to become a huge part of your income, in which case your ticket prices will be significantly higher and the experience will be different. It can be both a marketing and money-making exercise, just clarify that first up.

Then it's time to figure out how all of this is going to happen.

Plan

Planning is the detail-driven phase, when you assign your team and recruit volunteers, contract speakers, sponsors, venues and suppliers from styling to photographers and caterers.

Dive deep into run sheets and AV production like microphones, music, videos or slide presentations, perhaps even live streaming your event for people who can't attend in person.

Organise the travel, accommodation, freight and merchandise, which are the items you plan to sell at your event.

Complete the significant paperwork needed, from financials and budgets, to legals and contracts, to insurance and risk management.

Brand

This is where your audience starts to get the feel of your event through the event artwork, messaging, ticketing process and customer care, which are all part of the brand feel and experience.

Clear, consistent and beautiful branding that looks and feels professional will help you magnetise the audience effortlessly.

Launch

One of the most common mistakes to make with events is to focus on marketing and promo after the event has gone on sale. However, we want you to have all those marketing and promotional plans in place beforehand, helping you launch your event with anticipation, starting on a high with eager earlybird sales.

This is where you focus on PR, media releases and media relations. Have a clear strategy for TV, magazines or any long leads that need to be in place; promotions like social media campaigns; collaborations with aligned companies or influencers with the same values and interests.

It's also the time where you activate your audience and engage with your email community. Ensure they are receiving exciting correspondence and invitations. Roll out the red carpet for them, making them feel special with exclusive updates, bonuses and pricing.

Activating your audience to get out there and organically share their excitement about your event with their audience or friends is priceless.

Showtime!

Be organised with checklists and all the final preparations. Brief your team, speakers and sponsors. Remember that your event day is an awesome opportunity to create social media buzz!

Don't underestimate the power of comfortable shoes, maximum hydration and nourishment. These will help you stay calm and improve your troubleshooting skills.

Stay present, enjoy all your beautiful work and have fun!

Wrap

This is the final and most significant (yet underestimated) step to event success. Not only is it time to finalise the finances, thank your speakers and sponsors, and ensure all the loose ends are tied up, but this is your time to maximise audience connection and engagement.

Your audience has shared an incredible experience with you. Determine how you can support them in continuing the momentum of their experience. Nurture this new long-term relationship.

SELF-CARE ON THE ROAD

- **Know your limits!**
  Event days are filled with adrenaline, so make sure you're taking care of yourself in the lead-up (and the comedown). Add in the flights and air-conditioned hotel rooms and it can lead to exhaustion and burnout. Even though it's heaps of fun! Who knows how I used to add the booze into the mix too, during my old music touring days!
- **Simplify your rituals and take them with you**
  I've learnt to stick with morning meditation and some yin yoga stretches to music on my phone. Essential oils on the hotel pillow really help me sleep, because it smells like home.
- **Nourish yourself**
  When travelling, I always track down green veggie juices, eat extra protein, increase vitamin C and zinc, and roll diluted oregano, clove and cinnamon essential oils under my feet.
- **Schedule some bodywork**
  Chiro adjustments and massages after flights, events and heavy lifting make a world of difference too.
- **Recharge**
  I try to get plenty of alone time when I'm on the road to recharge. This can be hard when touring with people I love, as I want to stay up all night talking! I know now when to pull back.
- **Make sure others are looking after themselves too**
  Many of the event pros and speakers I have worked with are aware of their limits and requirements. An exhausted touring party is not a happy or efficient one.
- **Self-care, self-care, self-care**
  Take care of yourself and you will have a better experience ... and event!

~ SOULPRENEUR SUCCESS SUMMARY ~

✓ *Feel into what will take your business to the next level.*

✓ *Decide what your book/talk/event is about.*

✓ *Outline/plan your book/talk/event.*

✓ *Revisit your audience and take them into consideration in your writing/speaking/event angle.*

✓ *Understand how you will promote and launch yourself.*

✓ *Plan and execute the launch.*

✓ *Know yourself, know your limits.*

✓ *Surround yourself with your mindset tools and use your spiritual practice to have the courage and confidence to reach new heights.*

Closing Notes

Well, my new soul friend, it's time to turn your inspiration into action.

Whether you feel ready or not, because *you* might never feel ready, yet the world is more than ready for you. We've been waiting for you!

All journeys start with one step at a time. You could even start building a successful career or business implementing just one thing a day from this book.

Take what serves you, leave the rest behind, or come back to it later.

Most importantly never lose focus on why you were called to pick this book up and to start this journey in the first place. That magic which called from within you, and has been calling your whole life.

Believe in yourself. Have faith in your wings.

Know that your angels will catch and lift you.

Take risks, put yourself out there.

Have fun, fail fast and forgive yourself. You will learn more from failures and flops than any university degree.

You can always find your way back into alignment with what truly matters to you. Coming back stronger and wiser each time.

Identify when you are getting distracted, side tracked or losing your way. It happens. Just come back in ... again and again. Keep this book on your nightstand or in your handbag, pick it back up to re-read and remember who you are. It will always be here for you, to remind you of your inner power and magic.

Surround yourself with people and places who support the highest version of yourself. While holding space for your shadow when she needs her moment in the spotlight.

You do not need to be perfect. I don't know anyone who truly has all their shit together.

You have permission to change, to shapeshift. You do not have to stick to things that no longer serve you. Life's too short and sweet to stick to things for the wrong reasons.

Always remember that your wellbeing is the greatest gift you can give to those who love you.

Be kind, be gentle with yourself.

Ambition is a wild and wonderful thing, it will drive you and take you on a magical ride. Yet like all wild things, she will likely refuse to be restrained.

Remember to keep checking back in on where she is taking you, and why. Create a healthy and sustainable relationship with ambition. Be proud of your achievements, while ensuring they are aligned with your personal measurements of success and wellbeing.

Success for the sake of success does not lead to soul fulfillment.

Take your time, enjoy the ride and soak up every second.

How blessed are we to have the privilege to make our own decisions, to live life in our own way?! Let's use this privilege to light the way and create more opportunities for others to do the same.

I believe the world will be changed (for the better) when we have more power and prosperity in the hands of the lightworkers - that's you!

This is bigger than you may be able to fathom right now.

You taking your steps forward as a Soulpreneur is about so much more than you. Watch the ripple effect and beautiful influence you have on those around you.

So, let's go and reclaim your dreams and the life you were born to live.

Closing Notes

I can't wait to see you shine, I'll be right by your side, in the wings. No actually, I'll be front row, with pompoms. Watching your face light up when your angels whisper to you *"see, you had the magic in you all along"*
xo *Yvette*

P.S. Let's have fun doing this together in the book club: www.yvetteluciano.com/bookclub

I want to love each moment for what it is. I want to allow instead of resist. I want to float in the ocean. I want to sit among nature with nothing to do besides marvel at her beauty. I want to do things because I want to do them, not because I feel I 'should' do them. I want to wear my heart on my sleeve and be powerful in my vulnerability. I want to breathe deeply. I want ease and joy.

– Jess Ainscough

JOIN THE SOULPRENEUR BOOK CLUB!

Remember to unlock all your freebies, videos, audios and tools at: **www.yvetteluciano.com/bookclub**

You will also receive an invitation and link to join our online book club and connect with your fellow Soulpreneurs across the globe.

We will be inviting members to join us for Soulpreneur retreats, conferences and circles too – hopefully you can join us! Looking forward to connecting with you in there.

TO STAY IN TOUCH PERSONALLY

www.yvetteluciano.com • Facebook: yvettemluciano
Instagram: @yvetteluciano

Acknowledgements

In love and admiration of my husband, Isac. The most creative person I know, always colouring outside of the lines.

To my parents, Sylvia and Mark, for supporting me, standing by me and allowing me to find my own way to shine. And the rest of my family who have ridden big waves with me. Especially our newest little lightbeam, Leah Luciano, for lighting up my life right when I needed you most.

In honour of Louise Hay, and thanks to Reid Tracy, Leon Nacson, Rosie Barry and my Hay House family. You are the dream publishing home for *Soulpreneurs.*

To Gabby Bernstein, Sarah Wilder, Tallon Pamenter, Amanda Rootsey, Rachel MacDonald, Julie Parker and my Mysterymind sisters.

To Tara Bliss and my beloved Aroma Angels family and collaborators.

To Amy Cronin, Karla Pizzica, Shunanda Scott, Ros Scott-Mackenzie and our Soulpreneur community.

Nikita Byrnes for keeping me wild and truly free, Mardi Caught for being the wonder woman of the music industry, Tammy Hofbauer and Emmie Louise for being my first Soulpreneur sisters.

To my entourage of doctors and healers who have nourished my mind, body and soul over the years. For helping me thrive beyond all odds and expectations.

Acknowledgements

To everyone who has loved and supported me, especially through the darkest days and lowest moments when I'm certainly not my best or most soulful self, thank you.

To the yellow-tailed black cockatoos flying by, goannas across the way, faeries in the forest and all the elementals who graced my path and office window as I was writing this book.

To all the butterflies that surrounded me during the writing process, to remind me that my heavenly co-author was by my side. With so much gratitude for her, for the pages I don't even remember writing.

To Mount Coolum, as I watched you from my office window, honouring the journey we've been on in these years. You tested me, you grounded me, you humbled me, you elevated me.

Last but definitely not least, thank you Courtney Love, Björk, Brody Dalle, Nina Gordon, Louise Post, Melissa auf der Maur and all the musical goddesses and muses on repeat in the book writing cave.

We hope you enjoyed this Hay House book. If you'd like to receive our online catalog featuring additional information on Hay House books and products, or if you'd like to find out more about the Hay Foundation, please contact:

Hay House, Inc., P.O. Box 5100, Carlsbad, CA 92018-5100
(760) 431-7695 or (800) 654-5126
(760) 431-6948 (fax) or (800) 650-5115 (fax)
www.hayhouse.com® • www.hayfoundation.org

Published and distributed in Australia by:
Hay House Australia Pty. Ltd., 18/36 Ralph St., Alexandria NSW 2015
Phone: 612-9669-4299 • *Fax:* 612-9669-4144 • www.hayhouse.com.au

Published and distributed in the United Kingdom by:
Hay House UK, Ltd., Astley House, 33 Notting Hill Gate, London W11 3JQ
Phone: 44-20-3675-2450 • *Fax:* 44-20-3675-2451 • www.hayhouse.co.uk

Published in India by: Hay House Publishers India,
Muskaan Complex, Plot No. 3, B-2, Vasant Kunj, New Delhi 110 070
Phone: 91-11-4176-1620 • *Fax:* 91-11-4176-1630 • www.hayhouse.co.in

Distributed in Canada by:
Raincoast Books, 2440 Viking Way, Richmond, B.C. V6V 1N2
Phone: 1-800-663-5714 • *Fax:* 1-800-565-3770 • www.raincoast.com